SURVIVING RACISM

IN THE 21ST CENTURY WORKPLACE

"DISMANTLING THE DEI INITIATIVE"

By: Dr. Belinda Moore, Teacher, Author, Entrepreneur, Evangelist

The black woman's guide to identifying and overcoming racism, discrimination and harassment in the 21st Century workplace.

WWW.TRUEVINEPUBLISHING.ORG

"SURVIVING RACISM IN THE 21ST CENTURY
WORKPLACE"
By Dr. Belinda Moore

Published by
True Vine Publishing Co.
810 Dominican Dr.
Nashville, TN 37228
www.TrueVinePublishing.org

Printed in the United States of America—First printing.

FOREWORD

This book is dedicated to those individuals who have been victims of harassment, bullying, and discrimination in the workplace. The idea for this book came about naturally, as a consequence of my experiences after graduating from Court Reporting School in 1980. I was the only Black female in a class of all White females, and I embarked on the journey of integrating the judicial system—territory I had no idea would be so complex and, at times, hostile. I was stepping into what is considered "Holy Ground," where "In God We Trust" is etched on the walls and people are sworn to tell the truth and seek justice. I deeply appreciate my White colleagues who supported me wholeheartedly.

This book is a snapshot of the forty years I've spent as a Court Reporter Contractor. My business, Moore Reporting Services, has held numerous DEI-related contracts—before they were even labeled DEI—in state, local, and federal government institutions. These include the U.S. District Court in Tennessee (Joel Solomon Building), fifteen years with the Tennessee Valley Authority's EEOC Division, Labor Relations and Arbitrations Division, and Legal Division. For the State of Tennessee, I was awarded contracts with the Civil Service Commission of the Department of Human Resources for the entire state, the Department of Commerce and Insurance, and their Tenn Care Division. Additionally, I've held a six-year State of Tennessee contract as an Official Court Reporter covering four criminal courts with the Tennessee Supreme Court based in Nashville, Tennessee. I held that contract for 28 years. Also, an additional Beer and Wrecker Board contract, and a Merit Systems Protection Board contract; the City of Atlanta Traffic Court, the Fulton County Board of Education, and worked virtually in nearly every court in Atlanta, Georgia, and surrounding areas.

Long story short, this is what qualifies me to pen this book on dismantling DEI and its potential impact on small, woman-owned, disadvantaged businesses across the nation. This book shares the emotional toll of being victimized by those in power who resented my success and details some of the incidents that led to the loss of contracts—losses rooted not in performance, but in race.

TABLE OF CONTENT

CHAPTER 1

RACISM AND DISCRIMINATION

After thirty years of practicing in the field of court reporting, here I sit once again, pondering what's next for my business after losing three contracts to the blue wall of racism and discrimination. It didn't matter whether I was the low bidder or not, or that my performance had been rated excellent throughout the five- or six-year term of the contracts—I had no doubt that the non-renewals were because I was a Black woman who had become successful in business.

I was told that I "wasn't supposed to make that kind of money," and it became clear that those who served as gatekeepers over the day-to-day operations of the various departments had targeted my business for discrimination. Someone had taken it upon themselves to reverse the gains and achievements I had made, simply because they could— through racism and discrimination—knowing they would never be held accountable.

The judges received kudos, while my business was demoted—even after I had cleaned up a three-year backlog of transcripts left by the former White court reporter. That was the state of things when the contract was put back out to bid. I was the successful low bidder, and I caught up on all the outstanding transcripts. But now, with the backlog resolved, I was being terminated, and the contract was returned to the same White female who had previously failed to fulfill it.

I didn't know how I could manage to rebound from this. I didn't know if I even had the will or the strength to try. This wall—this impasse, this barrier—had been erected and has continued to raise its ugly head for the past thirty years.

I thought, should *I just retire and write about it? Maybe I can warn others in hopes of helping them as they walk down their own career paths—teach them how to navigate around and ultimately overcome the blue wall of racism. Because it is a reality.* The wall of racism and discrimination is real. Harassment and discrimination are the byproducts of racism. Without racism, there would be no harassment or discrimination.

I still don't know how I managed to survive what can only be described as *The Blue Wall*—a wall designed to impede and hinder me from becoming a successful, productive member of society. It left me to wallow in hopeless despair, stripped of vision and direction, as it attempted to slap labels on me: shiftless, lazy, trifling—

while denying the wall even exists. It takes a psychological and emotional toll. It wears on your psyche.

And to those small business entrepreneurs, I say this:

Keep pressing forward.

Don't give up.

Don't throw in the towel.

The only way to survive racism and discrimination in the workplace is to first admit it's real. But to admit the wall is a reality is to somehow have your patriotism questioned. It forces you into a vacuum of seclusion and dismay as you forge toward your destiny and purpose in mainstream corporate America—swimming upstream each year like the salmon, threading against a current that continues to deny you life, liberty, and the pursuit of happiness. A place in society. It all lends credence to the adage, *"America eats its own."* Swimming with sharks pales in comparison to surviving *The Blue Wall.*

My heart goes out to all those individuals who were never able to figure out what happened to them—those who are now despondent and somehow unable to articulate why things went so horribly wrong, or why they "went postal." Or like the young man at Virginia Tech who just snapped. He was unable to process what had happened to him, let alone know how to respond appropriately. He chose instead to act out in a horrific way—massacring his fellow classmates because he lacked the coping skills, the emotional mechanisms to process his hopelessness. Feeling betrayed because he was Asian, wandering aimlessly

9

through life—lost, never fitting in, ostracized, losing his identity—he was mocked and ridiculed, bullied because of his nationality.

Or the immigrant worker who, disillusioned and hardened by rejection, decides to become a professional criminal. He no longer cares what anyone says. He's chosen instead to set up a meth lab, becoming part of the local crime syndicate, working for the Cartel out of the backyard of his mobile home that sits just outside the local tent city. Now he sells drugs out the back door.

Or the Asian professional who feels invincible—believing the wall is only a figment of one's imagination. He believes that his education and intellect will ensure acceptance among his peers. But he, too, runs head-on into *The Blue Wall* of racism, hatred, and despair. Now tortured psychologically and emotionally to such an extent, he abandons his dreams of becoming a doctor of medicine and instead becomes a homicidal maniac—all because of his religious affiliation. We are seeing this played out more and more each day. The victims of *The Blue Wall* of racism come in all nationalities, races, and creeds.

The seasons of life constantly change, but *The Blue Wall* remains—a continuum of man-made obstacles designed to deter one from developing and building a thriving, bustling business at the level of success experienced by their White counterparts. The Wall is self-sustaining and self-perpetuating.

In 1976, I was the only Black court reporting student in my hometown. And now, in the year 2025, I remain the only Black court reporting entrepreneur—forty years later. Over the past forty years, however, every contract my business has ever been awarded has somehow been rigged and diverted to a White colleague—not because of the quality of my work, but simply, in their own words, because "we want our own." In other words, I was a Black woman-owned business in White corporate America, and they weren't ready to accept, let alone respect, a successful Black female entrepreneur—no matter how talented or gifted. The doors opened and closed constantly, with a revolving-door effect.

By the time I approached a six-figure income, some secretary, accountant, or jealous individual would become enraged at the fact that I was making more money than they were—and they would ignite a firestorm of discontent in the workplace. It took me a while to piece together what was happening. They were miserable in their $8.00 or $10.00 per hour jobs, while I was earning $65.00 an hour back in 1986. Their frustration mounted each time they saw the conference room door close, knowing I was on the other side. It reminded them that they had set their goals too low.

What's ironic is that the doors don't *have* to close— someone just chooses to shut them because they can. Some hater decides it's a great idea to destroy a Black woman's business, her dreams, her vision. *Who does she think she is, anyway? She's an uppity nigger.* That's

11

what I've experienced over the past forty years—without equivocation. And it's what qualifies me to author the first in a series of self-help books for Black individuals aspiring to reach the American Dream. I knew without a doubt that I had to persevere—again and again—and that failure was not an option.

That's why I say the Women's Movement did not include Black women or any women who weren't of Caucasian descent. It was developed by and for the benefit of White women. Whether or not Black women received an occasional perk, the truth remains: while some Black women participated in the movement, many of the same women who marched and protested back then have since become fierce competitors—or major detractors—of Black businesswomen. At least, that's been my experience over the past thirty years.

There's no real sister-girl camaraderie. Not much heartfelt support. Instead, it's a race to the finish line by any means necessary. And Rosa Parks was right—I've had many invoices go unpaid, tossed in the garbage to sabotage my ability to make payroll or retain staff. Now, in the 21st century, many successful Black women who have reached the finish line practice what I call *self-hate*. Rather than lifting one another up, they lash out, cursed by low self-esteem and resentment. Some go so far as to sabotage another Black woman's contract or spread false narratives, all to force her out of a courtroom or keep her from being recommended. Absolute power does indeed corrupt—even among powerful Black women.

Although doors have opened for *all* women, a Black woman's success is still viewed as minuscule in comparison to that of a Caucasian woman. The doors of privilege, opportunity, and entitlement do not swing open for Black female entrepreneurs. Instead, we face doors of skepticism, judgment, and criticism. Some Black women have shattered the glass ceiling, but they didn't take other sisters with them. Many fear competition and suffer from insecurity. And God forbid you're attractive—if the men in the courtroom paid you more attention than them, it was grounds for automatic termination. They would lie and stir up dissension to justify terminating your contract, knowing full well it was *they* who had the bad attitude. That's when I began documenting every instance of Black-on-Black discrimination in the workplace.

These constant, consistent acts of jealousy among Black women create cycles of short-lived success followed by devastating setbacks. We still see no Black women governors—and rarely any open acceptance of the very idea. In my town, here in the 21st century, there are no Black female or male judges, and only a few Black attorneys remain. Most will even refuse to take your case, even if you have a good one.

I'll never forget the day a White female accountant— who had never worked with a Black woman-owned business—made it clear she didn't appreciate me having a business at all. She decided, on her own, to change my invoice for a highly technical deposition—one that qualified for a higher pay rate. She changed it to whatever she wanted to pay, despite my explaining the process. As I reviewed the invoice at the front office counter—having come in to pick up my check—she reached over me, attempting to distract me from her attached letter explaining why she wasn't going to pay the full amount.

I stopped and said, *"Don't touch me!"* She was provoking me into a fight. She had already called around to my colleagues in the field, asking who I was, whether they knew me, and what they would have charged for the same job. This was as close to a fight as I had ever come—all over the idea of having to pay a Black person's invoice. Thank God for Rosa Parks' legacy—I had no idea it could be this bad. I found that many women don't play by the rules—not even the Rule of Law. They believe they are above it.

The very idea of a Black woman having a successful business disturbed her. And the fact that she had to pay me, that's the part she hated most. It was as though she'd taken some dark oath never to support a Black woman-owned business. She was offended by my success. That's when I fully realized what the Civil Rights Movement was about. Her actions said it all. And the look in her eyes—pure hatred and disdain—was chilling. It was the look of someone demon-possessed. She believed that, since I was Black, my work should be free.

One thing she made certain of: she was going to pay me *less* than what the job was worth. There was no *"Hello, I'm Susan. How are you today?"* No courtesy. Just pure disdain and gross disrespect.

She knew that once she finished adjusting my invoice to what *she* thought a Black person should be paid—as if we were haggling at a flea market—I'd leave her office angry, which is exactly what she wanted. She wanted to provoke me to a level of rage so she could call security and have me arrested for being "belligerent and threatening." All because she didn't want to pay me.

To this day, I still feel that if she could have, she wouldn't have paid me at all. I sensed the setup immediately—and if she could have had me arrested rather than pay me, she would have. But her provocation wasn't enough to cause me to lose my temper. I'll admit it—I was fuming, though. This was the first and only time in thirty years that someone had taken it upon themselves to adjust an invoice to whatever they wanted to pay.

As time passed, I consulted a lawyer regarding her actions and was informed that I had every right to set and demand a prevailing competitive wage for the work, as long as it wasn't unreasonable. Since it was my business and I was the owner, she had no right to change the invoice.

I once watched a telecast showing a lawyer being shot at by a client after stealing money from the client's trust account—because he could. Now he was being gunned down live on the 6 o'clock news. He turned out to be

15

nothing more than a two-bit thief, a criminal in a business suit. It was hard to feel sorry for him as he dodged bullets from behind a tree, trying not to get shot in the head by the very person he'd betrayed. He managed to avoid several shots before the client took off down the street, only to be caught by the police and placed in handcuffs.

After much reflection, I wondered if something had been triggered in her mind—perhaps from childhood. Maybe she had been raised to disrespect people of color. Her age suggested she had grown up during the Civil Rights era. To her, a Black woman asking to be treated with dignity and respect—and requesting that a check be ready upon arrival—may have infuriated her. She chose to interfere with my invoice instead, plotting her response in what became a power struggle, plain and simple.

On that day, I had just finished an assignment in Nashville and was headed home. I'd been in business for nearly thirty years at that point. And although more people had paid their invoices without issue than those who caused problems, this moment stood out. As I left the building's lobby, I noticed the security guard watching me carefully— making sure I exited the premises. That was part of her plan too, just in case I became "belligerent." She had deliberately provoked me, no doubt with the hopes of calling security to escalate the situation.

She had a plan. She got to adjust my invoice, physically provoke me, steal money from my business, and still have the potential to get me arrested. It made for quite a day. I chalked it up as a lesson learned and moved on.

Because of experiences like this, I once told my mother that I would never vote for a woman—president, governor, or anything else. Time had taught me that many women struggle to deal respectfully and forthrightly with other women. Too often, women scheme and connive against one another simply because they can. There's no real unity—at least not sincere unity. Many women secretly analyze, compare, compete, and tear each other down. I've never met as many discontent people as I've met in women who lack vision. Without vision, they create division and can't accept that the world isn't one-size-fits-all.

They upset the apple cart at every opportunity. And it's not *you* they have a problem with—it's *themselves*, for dreaming too small. If *you* have a purpose, it alarms them.

Entrepreneurs are born with a spirit of excellence. It's spiritual. I had a paper route at twelve years old and began understanding how money worked at a young age. And I've never seen so many discontent women trying to sabotage the destiny of others—they are miserable.

One thing is certain: a real woman—a *real* woman—will not sabotage another woman's business. She just won't do it. Most women who sabotage others suffer from a mental health disorder, in my opinion. I know what I've experienced. Most of them didn't even understand the business. They would sound the alarm: *"Court reporters make too much money!"* These were people just out of

17

law school, barely able to write an opening or closing statement—now claiming to be experts in court reporting.

Can't we all just get along?

My business has been sabotaged more than once by women with low self-esteem and low self-worth, who made it a competition. I lost a 15-year contract because of a Black female fresh out of law school who knew nothing about the field. Her only argument was that court reporters earned too much money. She undid the progress the EEOC had made in supporting qualified, diverse, woman-owned businesses. I was the only one in 1998—and in 2025, I'm still the only one in my hometown.

Being uniquely different often leads to being misunderstood. You're forced to survive each new episode of discrimination. You have to learn how to "rope-a-dope." You have to block punches and come back swinging. No other story illustrates the essence of *Surviving Racism in the 21st Century Workplace* quite like this one.

People are threatened by creative ability. Still, we are descendants of slaves. Our mothers' mothers picked cotton and raised the master's children—sometimes birthing one or two of their own. So when you seek respect, you often have to earn it the hard way—and demand that it be given.

As a Black woman-owned business, you will face astronomical hurdles, fences, and walls. You'll learn quickly that respect is rare, and haters are many—working to ensure your success is short-lived. Later, during seminary, I learned there's a term for this condition: *total depravity*—a depraved mindset.

Secretaries, legal assistants, and sometimes even lawyers will intentionally create problems in the workplace. Some will lie about receiving invoices—delaying payments by forty days or more—just to create dissension between the client and the contractor. Why? Because they resent you being paid at all. I call them *dream killers*.

It reminds me of that moment in the Rosa Parks movie when she registered to vote, and the clerk tossed her application in the trash. Then later, that same clerk denied ever having a problem with her. That's the issue—we allow broken, bitter people to destroy what the state is trying to build through Diversity, Equity, and Inclusion. These people have little true power, but they project what little they have by taking aim at Black business owners.

The root cause? They failed to dream. They're unhappy with themselves—not you.

Let me be the first to say, in my business, I've had many invoices go "missing" myself—and each time, I had to conduct extensive research to find out who the culprit was. More often than not, it was the secretary, the supervisor's assistant, the judge's assistant, or the administrator. For a small, minority, woman-owned business, this can be devastating. Not getting paid on time can cause you to lose employees, clients, and other essential personnel. But to the joker in the workplace, it's nothing more than a sick joke—a twisted game they've imagined in their own minds to feel superior. They never want to feel "less than" a Black woman, so they sabotage your business to feel relevant.

They resent the fact that you've dared to dream big—that your vision goes beyond a 9-to-5 job, something they never imagined for themselves. And now here you are, walking in your destiny, while they're stuck watching your invoices cross their desk. The only power they have is deciding whether or not to pass your invoice along to the finance department. And as the realization sets in that they set their goals too low, they lash out. For them, it becomes necessary to try and make you feel as bad as they do. Your success makes them feel inadequate—intellectually, emotionally, and psychologically. You're Black. You're not supposed to be intelligent enough to build a successful, technical, prosperous business. And now you've got the audacity to ask to be paid?

As a small business owner, intentional non-payment of invoices can be one of the most devastating setbacks you face. It becomes one of the hardest obstacles to overcome, as you're forced to make concessions for haters throughout your career—people who can't stand to see you get ahead. You'll have to bear the weight of other people's pain. Clearly, they are hurting, or they wouldn't do what they do. Haters are losers—that's why they operate the way they do. Mentally healthy people don't waste time trying to destroy someone else's business. Successful people don't get caught up in sabotage or office politics—they're too busy building, planning, and growing.

They see your letterhead, your income, and the high level of knowledge and expertise you bring to the table. That intimidates them. Suddenly, it becomes a full-fledged attack on you as a person and your business. Their only goal becomes ensuring their boss never uses your services again. This has happened to me at least five times—secretaries with no real skills but just enough access to get my business removed from the system. They feel I should be the one making the coffee, doing the copying, and cleaning the toilets—not them.

I remember one attorney who, in the middle of a deposition, told the secretary, "Let her make the copies"— referring to me. He believed the White female should be the court reporter, and the Black woman should be running errands. The room fell silent as he realized the secretary couldn't do my job. The truth was, she had no qualifications. She hadn't gone to school to be a court reporter—or anything else, for that matter. Her only real authority was opening the morning mail and answering the phones. But somehow, *I* had become the problem. The hate is self-perpetuating.

I've had this game played on me so many times, I've lost count. It's psychological warfare. I call it the *"Damsel in Distress"* game. She tells her boss, *"Oh, she keeps calling about a payment. I don't know what happened to her invoice! I don't even remember her sending one!"* Then she feigns hurt feelings: *"She was so rude. She hurt my feelings."* All of this drama is a performance designed to ensure your business won't be hired again—because she

21

doesn't have one. *"Please rescue me? Please help me deal with this Black woman?"* The old "Black person did it" excuse is still alive and well.

Over the past 30 years, I've had at least two attorneys join in on these games with their White female assistants. Rather than correct their employees, they jumped in and dismantled my business—directly participating in harassment and discrimination. But at its core, the question remains: Did you do your job and forward the invoice to the finance department thirty days ago? That's what it boils down to. They should have corrected their staff.

I must say, though—not one *male* judge has ever participated in harassment or workplace intimidation in the past 30 years. Even though they had the power, they respected the process, the Rule of Law, and took their oaths seriously.

Women write their own rules, rather than follow the Rule of Law.

In reality, the issue for many assistants is this: *"She makes more money than me. She owns her own business. I'm just a secretary with a job."* And from that place of resentment, they sabotage the relationship before it even begins. Every time you call, they're offended—as if your call interrupted some grand task. But what they're really saying is, *"I feel bad about my life, and I'm taking it out on you."*

These are just some of the yearly challenges that small, minority DEI businesses face. There is a constant power struggle.

And of course, when the invoice goes unpaid due to all the confusion, there's a strong chance your business won't be called back again—which is exactly what the secretary hoped for. She plotted and schemed for it from the outset. It's part of the larger game of devaluation.

To prove her loyalty and affirm his support for her, the boss often acquiesces to the whims of the "damsel"—not realizing the entire episode is a ruse. It's a sick, manipulative mind game from start to finish.

PLAYING THE HAND YOU'RE DEALT

PART 1

A nother instance, about thirty years ago, involved my business being awarded a major contract with the Board of Education to record student disciplinary tribunal hearings. A similar contract problem arose. I was being sexually harassed by the chairperson of the disciplinary tribunal. He held the fate of my business in his hands, and when he came on to me, I didn't know what to think—especially since he was a married man.

My business had been working with the Board for five years when the coordinator of student discipline decided to leave her post to become a homemaker and stay home with her children. The Board then hired a new coordinator, who in turn brought in a new secretary. The secretary was excited about her new position and pay scale, which she told me was either $8.00 or $10.00 an hour—mind you, this was back in 1987.

When my business's invoices started coming across her desk, she saw that I was earning $50.00 an hour for takedown only—which, at the time, was considered a high rate. This became a huge problem for her. She was clearly offended by my success.

Her desk sat right outside the hearing room door, and as soon as a hearing began, I'd get up and close the door—oh boy, was she upset about not making $50.00 an hour. She took it upon herself to start proofreading my transcripts, although this wasn't part of her job. She appointed herself as a gatekeeper, going on a fishing expedition looking for mistakes—any pretext to create friction and trouble in the workplace. If there was even one typo in a 200-page transcript, she'd use it to assert some false sense of superiority. Her behavior screamed of a deep inferiority complex.

She did just about everything she could think of to try to get me fired. She was fixated on those $50.00-per-hour invoices. Proofing my work was only the beginning. She constantly plotted and schemed to feel better about herself. It became clear she wasn't happy earning $8.00 or $10.00 an hour after all. She picked arguments over anything and everything, and my phone calls to the coordinator became opportunities for confrontation—her personal battleground. Most of the time, she was rude and disrespectful.

Eventually, we were both called into a meeting with the coordinator to discuss her contentious behavior and the growing difficulty in us working together. The meeting yielded nothing of substance—no discussion about workplace etiquette or mutual respect. She continued to walk around visibly offended, bloated with resentment, and emotionally swollen because I was in a better situation than she was. She wanted me to feel the same mental and emotional pain she was dealing with.

Her demeanor became increasingly unpleasant. When I came in for a hearing, she wouldn't speak—even when I greeted her first—and her eyes would pierce through me as I walked past on my way to the conference room. I considered it a hostile work environment. That, coupled with the tribunal chairperson's sexual advances and harassment, signaled to me that my time with the Board of Education was coming to an end.

Why didn't I tell the coordinator? Because doing so would have only compounded the problem and ended the contract even sooner. It became a matter of survival: report the conduct and face immediate unemployment, or tolerate it to keep the contract. Life is filled with hard choices. But workplace harassment—of any kind—should never have to be tolerated.

After two or three more meetings with the coordinator—and the secretary continuing to lie about whether I had called or followed up on business matters—she finally convinced the coordinator to stop using my services. Let that sink in: the *secretary* made that call.

It was apparent she was deeply unhappy with where she was in life and didn't know how to be happy for someone else who had worked hard to move past an $8.00-an-hour mindset and into an entrepreneur's mindset. The irony is, she had made those life choices—not me. Her situation had nothing to do with me. She had been born with what we call *White privilege*, yet she never truly utilized it. Her only use of the privilege was antagonism and self-pity over her own poor decisions.

Clearly, sabotaging someone with an entrepreneurial spirit was the only way she knew how to cope with her own mental pain. She knew asking for a raise would expose the jealousy driving her behavior. She had no real justification to ask for more money, and she knew she wasn't going to get $50.00 an hour. So instead, she chose harassment and degradation—which ultimately led to my dismissal after almost five years of service.

I called it *The Blue Wall of Racism*. Little did I know, there would be many more walls to tear down. But I was determined to push forward despite the setback my business experienced.

What's even more formidable is that many Black women have jumped on that same bandwagon—the bandwagon of envy, jealousy, and power struggles rooted in insecurity. When you tear down someone else just because they're successful, you're operating from a place of deep powerlessness. Some women do it to assert control, to make sure you know *they* are in charge. We've become our own worst enemies.

Others do it out of low self-esteem or lack of self-worth. I considered this whole experience a life lesson—and moved on to the next chapter of my life.

PLAYING THE HAND YOU'RE DEALT

PART 2

All throughout the time I had worked for the Board of Education, I also had a bid on another contract with the City of Atlanta's Traffic Court, recording DUI hearings and jury trials on vehicular homicide cases or deaths by traffic accidents. In 1997, I was awarded that contract, earning $65.00 an hour—an impressive rate, especially for a Black woman-owned business. I considered myself a trailblazer. At the time, there were maybe five Black women in the entire city working in the field; they would be considered my competitors. Everyone else was White.

Trying to grow the business and bring in as many fresh faces as I could, one Black colleague I didn't know personally called and asked if she could work with me and help cover some of the jury trials. She submitted her résumé, and because I occasionally needed backup, I welcomed her in. At the time, that was something I would have appreciated—support and opportunity. We could both make money and avoid struggle.

After about two months of no contract work—and curiously, no follow-up from her—I called the courthouse to check in. To my surprise, I was told she had submitted a bid and undercut me at $55.00 an hour. The contract was now hers. The city simply stopped calling my business.

The lesson I learned? It's difficult for two Black women to work together in this space. It builds fences—not walls, but fences. She didn't keep the contract beyond six months and eventually moved to another courthouse position—but not before she caused a major disruption to my business. I had to reinvent the wheel all over again.

And to that, let me just say: when state, federal, and local DEI contracts are established and those in power witness Black people fighting over contract work, disrespecting one another, it sends a ripple effect. It becomes Black-on-Black discrimination. It impedes progress. Betrayal and distrust within the community are things we must own and address.

What's ironic is that even when I paid employees $13.00 an hour for straight typing, some still wanted to be me. They focused only on the bottom line—what I was charging the agency—coveting my success. I had one employee who only proofread transcripts say to me, *"I ain't gonna help you make all that money."* She resented her role and had no skills outside of reading and finding errors. I had to let her go. It was a one-sided working relationship. As her employer, I had helped her move at least three times from apartment to apartment, and had been her taxi on many, many occasions. It was clear to me that she was jealous, and would rather be broke than help me make all that money, as she put it.

It never failed, my business would experience spurts of enormous growth, and just at the time the business was about to take off, someone would step up and say, *"You make too much money,"* or, *"We want our own."* I'd have to restructure or redesign my entire business plan at a moment's notice just to keep it up and running.

No one can ever prepare you for the disloyal colleagues or the invisible wall that's there — the game and the wall you can't see, but it remains impenetrable by most. It's not for the faint of heart. It's difficult to fight in a game, as there generally is no rhyme or reason for its existence in the first place, except in the mind of the gamer. However, one thing is certain: you quickly find out who your true friends are.

Reality is truth. The game? Fiction.

However, this game is rooted in deception—a lie about the American Dream. Many Black people deceive themselves. They want the spotlight but lack wisdom. They crave success but lack the integrity and character to maintain it. They'll destroy one another to get to the top but can't stay there. This is the sin nature in all of us.

The wall has been fortified for decades—since the sit-ins and Civil Rights demonstrations of the '60s. It's so entrenched that even your own mother and father didn't know what to say to help you leap over it. So they prayed for you. Thank God for the courage and determination of people like Rosa Parks and Dr. Martin Luther King, Jr.

It is indeed a fact that, on every DEI contract I've held, I've experienced invoices being thrown in the garbage, intentional delays by purchasing departments, or delays when being sent to accounts payable for processing.

Surviving the wall is for over-achievers—not under-achievers.

Complainers sit on the sidelines, criticizing others because they can't figure life out for themselves. They harp on your accomplishments because they have no vision or career of their own. I call them losers. That's what losers do—point out flaws in someone else's business while building nothing of their own. They say things like, *"I'll give it two months." "It won't last."* Then they watch you stay in your rented office space for ten years—and they're in awe.

They're sellouts—because they never planned to go to college, and now resent the fact that you have five degrees. Losers love shortcuts. Like desktop icons, they've mastered the art of shortcuts to success—living paycheck to paycheck and stepping on whoever gets in their way. They pretend to be knowledgeable, but they're functionally illiterate in the world of business.

Don't let yourself become a victim of the complainers.

That's why every time I was awarded a contract, I didn't announce it. I functioned quietly. If the complainers had known, they would've called someone in the city, county, or federal offices to try and divert the contract away from me—simply because they didn't understand my industry or didn't want me to succeed. Many of them didn't even know how to start a small business.

To that end, I say: If you have a vision for a new business—**don't tell anyone.**

Keep it to yourself.

I learned the value of silence. Let them remain ignorant and uninformed—that's how you survive. People without vision cause division—whether in families, workplaces, or churches.

Surviving the wall is for people of character and integrity—not liars, cheaters, or thieves.

It's for risk-takers, not cowards. It's for trailblazers. For the prepared—not the unskilled or unlearned.

Is it any wonder so few people succeed as small business owners? Some fall into what used to be called *Uncle Tom* behavior—selling out others for personal gain. Biblically, we'd call that spirit *Judas*. Judas was a person of color—Black. But make no mistake, Judases come in all races, creeds, and colors.

Across ten to twenty contracts in over forty years, my haters couldn't understand why I was so blessed. The truth? I never told them my strategy. I didn't share how much I made or how my business operated. It wasn't their business. And yet, the American Dream became a reality for me through hard work and determination. I didn't have to sleep my way to the top.

Over the past forty years, I've seen and heard it all. Conspiracy theorists united in an effort to remove me from contracts—based solely on the color of my skin. Many Black people never reach this level of awareness. But I believe I was *chosen* for this assignment—this mission.

In 1977, I was the first Black person to enter the field of Court Reporting. After a short-lived marriage of just 11 months—forced upon me due to pregnancy after being assaulted in high school—I was determined to reclaim my life. My innocence had been stolen, and I wanted it back. I graduated high school, divorced, and refused to compound that mistake. I refused to wallow in self-pity.

And guess what? Eventually, I won.

Here it is now, some fifty years later, and I've bought two homes and five Mercedes-Benz vehicles. That innocent young girl, whose future was once stripped away, now has it all back again. I can truly say—it was all worth it. Looking back, I was a straight-A student, a rising star. Since then, every good decision I've made has been with premeditated intent—never to become a victim again. To that I say: *refuse to play the victim.*

On my Department of Human Resources contract, one of the judges looked down the table at me during a hearing and said, *"You come all the time!"*

Translation: *"I really don't want you here."*

He hadn't been told that it was a DEI contract, and that the State was working to help develop small, woman-owned and minority businesses. I didn't have the luxury of

a team at the time, so I had to fulfill the contract myself—
or risk losing it. In truth, he was coveting my income
and distracted by my presence. I wasn't trying to corner
the market. But had I not shown up, it would have been
flagged as a performance issue. There was no such thing
as "reverse discrimination," as some had implied. I was
simply the only Court Reporter out there in a niche most
Black professionals didn't even know existed.

In another hearing, yet another lawyer looked at me and
said, *"We want our own!"*—not realizing that the city had
sought out small, Black, disadvantaged businesses to fulfill
DEI (or, at the time, affirmative action) obligations. I just
happened to be—and still am—the only Black-owned court
reporting business in my hometown. Like in school, I was
the only Black student in the class, and I had no idea of the
level of hatred and discrimination I would face stepping into
an all-White judicial system. I was apprehensive, yes—but
I had the courage to keep going, no matter what it took.

In another instance of blatant racism, the attorney who
contracted my business to appear in court informed me that
the judge told his secretary to tell the attorney:

"Don't bring that nigger back in my courtroom!"

That was around 1996. And I don't believe for one
second that the complainers—the losers, rather—could
have endured the mental pain and anguish that comes with
being a small Black woman-owned business chosen by
God to integrate the judicial system. That's why I refused

to share any of the details with the unlearned and ignorant. *Talk is cheap.*

The secretary could barely speak as she repeated what had been said to her. She was visibly shaken and simply wanted me to know what the judge had instructed. I was speechless. I felt bad that she had to carry that message. Still, the wall of hatred persisted.

And yet—I went back into that same courtroom on another occasion, and the judge didn't have me escorted out either. Maybe he'd had a *come-to-Jesus* moment and repented, realizing the courtroom is meant to be a holy place where people seek *justice*, not *just us.*

I tell you: the wall is not a myth. It's a reality.

And I submit—it's harder to fight reality.

You ask yourself, *Whatever happened to the content of one's character?*

Whatever happened to being judged on proficiency, dependability, and reliability?

We've come a long way since Dr. Martin Luther King Jr.'s *"I Have a Dream"* speech—yet today, that dream has been reduced to a fanciful notion. Many have thrown in the towel on DEI and affirmative action initiatives—and who could blame them? Especially when they witness two DEI hires fighting in the workplace over who gets the promotion, even when one clearly didn't earn it. She slept her way into the position.

Here I am in the 21st century—the first African American court reporting agency in my hometown and in my state. The first to have the idea. The first to dream it. The first to penetrate the blue wall of justice and learn the actual bidding process. And yet—I still can't work in any court in the city where I live.

I fought hatred and discrimination for many years, until finally, one day, I was contacted by the federal court system in my state and asked if I'd be interested in bidding on a DEI federal court contract.

Translation: They needed a small, disadvantaged, minority business. All White court gives the overt appearance of the impropriety of racism.

By that time, my business had begun taking on medical dictation contracts with the state, and this opportunity with the U.S. District Court felt like a step in the right direction. I saw it as a way to fully return to my career field. I jumped at the chance.

By then, I'd learned not to tell a soul—and I didn't. I allowed the ignorant to remain ignorant as I forged ahead with new vigor and determination. I didn't want to be distracted by the *peanut gallery*—the ones who'd carry back negative feedback, misinformation, and spin to the community at large. They were the ones without vision— the ones who caused division centered around your goals, your dreams, and your aspirations.

PLAYING THE HAND YOU'RE DEALT

PART 3

Nowadays, we live each day watching people jump over the edge of the cliff. Virginia Tech and Fort Hood are perfect examples—tragedies where individuals, unable to leap over the blue wall of hatred and disrespect, were impacted so deeply that, while suffering from PTSD and manic depression, they chose suicide. In their pain, they lashed out, massacring those they believed played an integral role in their downfall—for whatever reason.

Many people have given up on the idea of becoming business owners altogether, and I believe that's by design. When too much pressure is placed on a visionary, they begin to doubt their vision entirely. I've seen people give up—losing the faith to step out and believe in something greater than a job mentality. The oppression can be devastating, especially when you're struggling just to put food on the table and pay the mortgage each month. Meanwhile, people work to keep you in a place where they can manage you, daring you to dream at all.

You're constantly barraged with the message: *Get a good education and you'll get a good job.* But upon graduation, if there is a "good" job out there, the gatekeepers of the wall will make sure your name isn't on it. The system promotes DEI programs but fails to inform their own gatekeepers of their mission, so you're continually targeted with strife in the workplace. And if you defend yourself, that defense becomes the very excuse used to dissolve the contract that took you years to secure.

It reminds me of the time when the judge's secretary became so jealous that I received a promotion, and I was Black, sitting in an elevated seat on the left side of the judge, that she actually took a swing at me from the floor. And of course, I stated, *"bring it!"* The judge witnessed this. And wouldn't you know, the zero tolerance policy against violence in the workplace didn't apply to her secretary, but eventually they worked in concert to terminate my 28 year contract. The person that ended up with my promotion just happened to be the judge's secretary's friend.

On several occasions, gatekeepers became envious and jealous of the state, city, or county governments that attempted to support small minority businesses. They would set you up—similar to the situation Rosa Parks faced at the voting administration. In the 21st century, one thing is certain: even if the gatekeeper is wrong, the system will support them in terminating your contract.

Many years ago, when I was just a child, I watched my grandfather and grandmother work at a company called Crane Enamel for over thirty years, with the expectation that they would retire with dignity.

Now, people go from job to job to job, over and over, just to survive. There's rarely enough stability to buy a home, let alone the car of your dreams—or to plan for a secure retirement. People have become hungry and destitute. By no uncertain terms, people are desperate.

Yes, we live in a time of disposable people. A time when people are out for themselves—selfish, greedy, ambitious. We live in a time and space where many are so desperate for basic necessities that they'll stoop to anything—murder, Ponzi schemes, selling drugs, meth, crack—all sorts of devices, all because the wall has shut them out.

Because of this unwillingness to accept others—this shutting out—we are now living with crime-ridden, crime-infested pockets across society, across all races. People live in deplorable conditions because of the invisible blue wall of exclusion. There are entire sections of towns and cities where you won't find us after sundown—day or night. They call them *"Sundown Towns"*—places that are still bloodthirsty, where people are willing to kill at the drop of a hat.

It's a form of insanity that no one wants to address—for fear of retaliation. Many of our communities resemble third-world countries because no one wants to see others living in abundance. In this country, striving for the pursuit of happiness is easier said than done—and living peaceably with neighbors seems like a far-fetched dream.

People are in such despair that they lack respect for one another and will step on—and step over—each other in order to survive. We're living in desperate times. Surviving the blue wall is a tremendous feat, especially with the unemployment rate looming, as people reflect on what matters most in their lives: survival and self-preservation.

It's survival of the fittest, while political protesters boldly carry signs for your children to see—signs that reinforce your dilemma: *"We want our own!"* *"We want our country back!"* These are reminders that you are not welcome, that you are not a part of this country—you simply don't belong here. These signs are hard to miss, implying that you have no right to the American Dream, let alone life, liberty, and the pursuit of happiness. People aren't just falling off the edge; they aren't just "going postal" due to mental illness from their workplaces—they're being driven to the brink of insanity by what they've uncovered behind the blue wall: a devastating miscarriage of justice and a flagrant violation of the Constitution of the United States of America. These people just snapped.

When faced with the wall, your heart pounds, your palms sweat—you panic at the thought of not being able to survive. A surge of negative energy sweeps over your body, reminding you that you're standing in quicksand—and sinking fast. It's like a powder keg, ready to explode, fueled by the urgency of the matter. Crime is surging, and hate spews up like a volcanic eruption across this nation.

We're living in a time of deep uncertainty and hopelessness. We're afraid to leave our homes at night. We fear being robbed during the day, maimed or murdered, even while we sleep—locked behind metal bars we've installed on our doors and windows in the name of safety. It's a type of self-inflicted prison we've built for ourselves, all while being bombarded with pharmaceutical ads promising to invigorate our sex lives.

Is it any wonder why there are so many sexually transmitted diseases plaguing society today—diseases that are slowly but surely leading us to self-destruction—while the pharmaceutical industry continues to invent new drugs to help us cope with the consequences of our insatiable appetite for sexual pleasure? Our obsession with sex has now left us with life-threatening STDs across the planet. Sex is a great gift from God when used appropriately. But in this country, it seems all roads lead to illicit sexual behavior.

The prisons are overflowing with inmates, so much so that states have begun eliminating the burden placed on them by the penal system, as the cost of housing inmates continues to skyrocket—surpassing the cost of a college education—so states are releasing prisoners back into an already fragile and struggling society.

What a hard lesson to learn: It is better to educate, train, and strengthen a society—reinforcing the individual—

than to allow someone to become inmate number 456 in pod 789 at your local or state maximum-security prison. This system has now become a multi-billion-dollar-a-year industry—the infamous pink elephant. That's what I call running headfirst into the blue wall. But now it's too much, too little, too late. We've grown far too comfortable with the idea of reintegrating inmates into society without ensuring they have proper support from stable family systems, churches, or employers. Without that support, another innocent bystander is likely to become a statistic of a senseless, random crime.

Frankly speaking, because many inmates lack the skills, knowledge, and education necessary to survive in today's tough economic climate, we should at least offer those who are willing and psychologically stable the opportunity to enlist in the military. Let them become productive members of society while earning a paycheck and training to become soldiers—free soldiers, not angry, bitter, unproductive men with too much time on their hands. What a powerful testimony it would be: "I was once an inmate who took advantage of a military or prison release program—now let me show you how I became a man." Personally, I believe some males simply take longer than others to grow up and stop rebelling against authority. But many can still become resourceful members of society.

Upon release, and after a thorough psychiatric evaluation and a sufficient period of observation during incarceration, those inmates deemed qualified by the warden should have the option of joining a branch of the military. That should be a viable path—specifically for those who want to make a difference. There are ways to make amends; they just have to step up and take advantage of the opportunity.

When an inmate is released, they should be capable of entering the workforce—especially in the sectors where they are needed most and can make a meaningful impact. As they grow into manhood, they must learn there is more to life than the "box" or "pod" they've considered home for most of their adult lives. They should be taught the very basics of survival and how to earn an honest living.

Any branch of the military could serve as a powerful environment for the former inmate to grow and develop, rather than allowing our jails to remain overcrowded with people convicted of petty crimes—people who could otherwise become instruments of military excellence while fighting for a cause. That's what's missing. We're leaving our youth and young adults to fend for themselves. The lack of strong, positive role models is a leading cause of their demise. Men beget men. Being mentored by strong male role models could truly turn their lives around and transform them into productive members of society. We should consider reinstating the draft.

Perhaps assigning one reformed inmate to two or three strong sergeants could help reinforce and cultivate an atmosphere of manhood in a structured training environment. This would not only promote self-reliance and self-esteem—it would help these individuals appreciate the new roadmap they've been given.

Upon release, there should be more than just a work release program monitored by half-hearted, overburdened parole officers, many of whom work for a state prison system that lacks sufficient staff to provide adequate support for formerly incarcerated individuals. An inmate's release should address the core issues of their being—mind, body, and soul—rather than merely focusing on ankle monitors, check-in dates, and random drug tests. Instead of being cast into environments void of guidance and direction, they should be released into spaces of empowerment, employment, self-worth, and hope—not hopelessness and recidivism. Until the male-dominated species becomes more than a castaway left to his own devices, society will continue to deteriorate. There is no true awareness of self without the Word of God.

Many people lack self-awareness—an understanding of their identity in Christ—in a world that continues to refuse to acknowledge them as relevant. So I speak into the atmosphere: **You are relevant!**

Far too many have been forced to choose between what's ethical and humane, and what is unjust and immoral, simply to survive and put food on the table. It's a tough price to pay. Some choices cost too much—the cost exceeds the benefit. And in the case of Black communities, the "house Negro" is often destructive to the "field Negro." This isn't a myth. The house Negro is threatened by the perceived independence of any other Black individual—not just the field hand. This dynamic is still alive in the 21st-century workplace. I've seen educated Black professionals fighting other Black professionals simply because they became successful. It's a power struggle.

Sure, we're proud of our Generation X and Z college graduates from Morehouse and Spelman. But when they step into the real world, I've seen firsthand—in my own business—that some have an issue with someone making more money than them. One graduate once said to me, "Court reporters make too much money." She clearly coveted the fruits of my business without understanding the process it took to get there.

I had been with that company for fifteen years. She would have still been in middle school by the time my business began earning a profit after years of foundational work. I lost that contract by default—because of the ignorance of another Black woman. I had been sought out by the DEI initiative (formerly Equal Opportunity), offered the contract, and was fully primed, trained, and equipped to perform—with no complaints. Then along came this uninformed woman, jealous of my income, who got the contract terminated. Dr. Martin Luther King Jr. was right: a threat by anyone who doesn't know Christ is a threat to everyone who does. Uncle Tom-ism is not dead.

What's ironic is, she didn't understand the scope of work or how challenging the contract was to fulfill. She was new to the position and didn't realize I had to drive over

200 miles most mornings to get to the job site, often paying out-of-pocket for gas and hotels to ensure my presence the next morning. She ended up crippling the agency—at the time, the EEOC of a major power company—which had engaged competent small businesses through an incubator program to meet DEI compliance initiatives. A couple of years later, after realizing no one else wanted the contract because it was so difficult to manage, she offered it back to me. I declined. She had to figure it out on her own.

When she was in middle school, I was out there kicking down walls of hatred and discrimination, blazing trails— only to be shut out by someone of my own race, a woman more than a decade younger, who lacked the wisdom and understanding of the work. And to be clear, there was no performance issue—just a woman's issue. This was the second time a graduate from a historic HBCU undermined my business without knowing the scope of the work or understanding the business structure. Her only issue? I made too much money. Interestingly enough, she never made the same comment about my White colleagues.

She had a job mentality. That generation stepped into a world with all the doors wide open. And while that can be honorable, there's a price to pay. Uncle Tom-ism, discomfort around successful peers, and jealousy have set Black progress back. We disrespect one another, create unnecessary workplace drama, and let power struggles dominate spaces that should be collaborative. These issues create setbacks that could otherwise be avoided. The truth

47

is: **power cannot erase how you see yourself**—your self-worth, your low self-esteem.

Can you imagine the mental anguish one must feel to intentionally sabotage someone else's destiny? That's a red flag. That level of malice reveals deep self-hatred.

Your success makes them feel small and insignificant. And that, right there, is one of the reasons why more Black professionals haven't made it. It's a Black power struggle—a subculture within a culture. Why? Because it's a kind of tunnel vision. Some believe this is what the system wants from them—that showing loyalty to "the agency" means shutting down another Black business. That's why they do it—to curry favor with *massa*. That kind of thinking—that *stinking thinking*—has derailed the future of many small minority-owned businesses. It's nothing short of Black-on-Black crime in the workplace.

The irony of it all is, that the system finds it difficult to cultivate and build winning teams of employees when there's infighting among Blacks. The system generally allows it to play itself out, as they don't know how to address Black-on-Black workplace harassment, intimidation, and bullying. It's complicated. Often, this is learned behavior—driven by the need for self-preservation and self-worth—coupled with selfish ambition and a type of paranoia that stems from personal fear and low self-esteem. These become the catalysts for why some Blacks target one another in the workplace.

It's not exclusive to Blacks—Whites practice this behavior too—but not nearly as frequently or as destructively.

When looked at holistically—and Biblically—it's a symptom of total depravity, a residual effect from the fall of humanity in the book of Genesis. Cain killed Abel for these same reasons. He looked over and thought, "God accepted your offering, but rejected mine." Cain represents the enmity between the Devil's seed and Eve's seed. God corrected Cain, saying, "If you do well, I will accept your offering too." But Cain was cursed and banished into an alternate reality for the rest of his life. The key phrase: "If you do well."

So when we encounter these individuals in the workplace, it's no surprise what's going on within them. We live in a fallen world, full of fallen people, all trying to coexist by any means necessary on this planet. It was a tough lesson for my business to learn. I hope that, by writing this book, you'll begin to see people for who they are and judge them by their actions. You'll begin to understand why they do what they do.

We're often threatened by those who don't have an identity crisis—by those who are confident, clear, and more successful than we are. Their presence makes others feel uncomfortable. The mindset of the 21st-century Black job-seeker is: *"You're doing better than me? Then I'll hold you down."* I dare you to ask any corporate Black professional in America whom they've helped obtain gainful employment in the past five years—no, in the past two years. Ask who they've referred, interviewed, or were even offered an opportunity to support them. In most cases, the answer will be: no one.

The fierce competitiveness and fear of losing their job outweighs their willingness to help, even when they know someone is qualified. And more often than not, these same individuals have incited workplace drama, participated in terminations, or contributed to others being laid off. Like racism, Uncle Toms are not dead—they are alive and well.

This confusion in the workplace is one reason we see constant turnover. It's a type of baggage that has plagued Black Americans since slavery and continues into the 21st century. That should really make you stop and think. These individuals have no peace within.

Corporate Blacks can even engage in genocidal tactics. It's as if they must lash out at someone—but rather than challenge their White counterparts, they target the most vulnerable link: another Black person. I've been on the receiving end of this more times than I can count. They've been under pressure to appear loyal to the status quo, and every chance they get, they undermine a fellow brother or sister. They feel that they must destroy someone to survive. This is displaced self-worth. It's self-hate. They don't even realize that what they're doing is evil, unethical, and morally wrong.

Blacks focus on each other rather than the task at hand. Instead of fostering teamwork, they create strife and dissension in order to get ahead. When someone else brings real talent to the table—especially talent that rivals or exceeds theirs—it disturbs them. There's a preoccupation with status, and a deep lack of appreciation for one another.

Corporate Blacks often see themselves as enforcers of the underclass. They become **self-appointed assassins** of their own people, believing that by tearing others down, they secure their own place. They stand back asking, *"Am I my brother's keeper?"* But the fear of receiving a RIF (Reduction in Force) notice—or becoming just another unemployed Black person—petrifies them. So they play the game by any means necessary, casting aspersions and leaving casualties of war across the agency. Their fear of someone else's success is greater than their sense of justice or community. Deep down, they know: *I could be next.*

On a personal note, corporate Blacks still hate in the 21st century. When they see another Black contractor who doesn't speak Ebonics or who acts "ghetto"—someone who presents as a true professional—they feel threatened. If you appear more independent from the system than they are, you remind them that they are still trapped by it. While you may be thinking outside the box, they *are* in the box— the gatekeepers. They represent the division that awards contracts and determine how high or low you can go within the agency.

I've heard it more times than I care to count: *"If you're a contractor, you're an outsider."* To them, they're inside the system you've managed to leap out of—and your success makes them uncomfortable.

The gatekeepers determine whether your invoices are paid on time and whether they even make it to the finance department or accounts payable. When they don't, it can prevent you from making payroll, buying supplies, or even accepting new assignments—all due to the deceitfulness of someone who is supposed to process your paperwork. What they don't say is often more important than what they do say. They won't admit, "I have a job mentality, not an entrepreneurial spirit." They won't say, "I feel awful about my lot in life, and now this Black person walks in with a six-figure contract award." Instead, they subvert and divert your paperwork—and the money that's been set aside by the government for the advancement of small businesses. In the 1980s, they called them *set-asides*—contracts reserved for small, woman-owned Black businesses.

As a small business owner, you wear many hats. And I'd say to anyone: if you're going to make it, you'll have to fight the gatekeepers just to keep going. Gatekeepers come in all races and colors. And quite honestly, they are some of the unhappiest people I've met in the business world. It's almost as if they expect you to apologize for being successful. To that, I say—**hogwash**!

Rather than do their jobs in the purchasing department and award you the $200,000 contract your business has qualified for—and rightfully earned—some Blacks in government will use their internal power to push you out, defame your business, and block the support systems put in place through Set-Asides, Affirmative Action, EEOC, and DEI programs. These initiatives were created specifically to support small, minority-owned businesses. Over the past thirty years, the names have changed, but the purpose remains: to provide a good-faith effort to help disadvantaged entrepreneurs.

Here's something I'd say to the government—something I've never heard said before: *If you're going to award contracts that support women-owned businesses, you must also train and inform your gatekeepers. Make them aware of the mission. Hold them accountable for how they interact with vendors.* One of the biggest obstacles I encountered with contracts was that the gatekeepers were often devious and envious. They felt slighted—because they never dared to dream big themselves—and so they would sabotage the contractor's success.

There should not only be checks and balances when Black people are at the helm, but there should also be a mandate: *support qualified contractors.* The lie they often tell is that these contracts are being given to unqualified businesses. That's not true—it's just a convenient excuse. The reality? Many Blacks simply hate seeing other Blacks prosper. It's a tragic mindset—perhaps part of some deeply rooted curse for worshipping idols or false gods. I haven't met a Black person yet who could consistently celebrate another Black person's success without bringing up gossip, misinformation, or slander—and I was the one paying their salary! It's an inferiority complex. It's jealousy, plain and simple.

I had to fire at least three Black women who worked for me for that exact reason. It was clear—they were jealous of my success. Bewildered that **they** weren't in power. Upset it wasn't one of their relatives. Angry that they weren't the ones receiving the benefits. It's not their business—but the thought of your business making more money than they've ever dreamed of, while they're barely making rent, becomes a stumbling block.

So rather than celebrate your growth—hiring new employees, renting office space—they sabotage it. They block you from getting that $200,000 contract, even though you're qualified. All while holding a $40,000-a-year government job and enjoying federal insurance—yet they're holding your business hostage. We can't blame everything on racism. The onus is also on Black people to stop hating one another. Stop discriminating out of jealousy and envy.

Some of them are so desperate to please *massa* that they think it's their duty to withhold the contract from you—as if that's what *massa* wants. But in reality, it was the DEI division in their own agency that sought you out as a qualified contractor. After you've worked your way to the top, the gatekeeper is now standing at the entrance blocking your path. We need to stop promoting the false narrative that contracts are being given to people who aren't qualified – that's not true in 99 percent of the cases. However, there are some anomalies.

They're looking for brownie points—maybe even hoping for a promotion. I've lost at least five DEI contracts because of women with low self-esteem and low self-worth, who simply weren't comfortable seeing me in the right place at the right time. The truth is—it was earned.

They desperately await their *attaboys* from *da'massa*—dutifully patrolling the workplace, thinking they're helping the system by sabotaging the contractor that the agency *chose*. In doing so, they're promoting and perpetuating racism and discrimination in the workplace—and the saddest part is, they're Black just like you.

This is the most power they will ever have over you, so they stack the deck against your business to empower themselves. You've already passed a government clearance, but now they're digging into your background to uncover some past youthful indiscretion. Sadly, they didn't realize I was the glue holding 22 judges' schedules together—cleaning up the three-year backlog left by the previous contractor. With my expertise, skill set, and dependability, I managed to clear nearly four years of backlogged transcripts left behind by the prior court reporter who had done an awful job. The contract came up for bid, and my business was awarded the contract. After cleaning up her mess and earning kudos from the commissioners, the judges were finally back on track.

Then the new Director of Personnel, a former HBCU student arrived—fresh out of law school with an entry-level degree and no knowledge of the department's history or the Human Resources department's structure. Without any understanding of what had come before, and driven by jealousy and ignorance, she disrupted the entire system.

Once the contract was taken from me, things unraveled quickly. Within two years, the judges were backlogged again. Transcripts were scattered across multiple agencies, none of which cared whether they were completed on time or not. The system regressed. And who got the blame? The very same Director of Human Resources who had terminated my business. Ironically, she sent me the contract again to rebid, but I refused. I wasn't about to go behind another White firm and clean up their mess. Not again. They drove a hard bargain, and a higher prevailing wage. And since that time, I've worked with judges who've shared that after COVID happened, that department completely fell apart, meaning that karma finally caught up with the Director of the department.

She hadn't understood how the Department of Personnel worked. She'd walk into the hearing room, and seen that I was the only other Black person present sitting around the commission table, and felt the need to assert herself. She wanted to be the last woman standing—intoxicated by her new title as an Attorney Director, fresh out of college, but with absolutely no clue of how the contract process worked, she terminated my contract.

Similarly, another so-called sister—another HBCU grad—transferred into a major power company's EEOC division where I had worked with that agency for 15 years.

She came into the EEOC division, where I'd built strong working relationships with investigators and labor relations staff, even working with judges flying in from Washington, D.C. to preside over hearings. And yet, this entry level attorney, having no knowledge of the department or the scope of work required, chose not to renew my contract. She ended 15 years of loyal, dependable service, just because she could.

Women like this come with an axe to grind. She didn't even try to understand the work. Instead, she said, "Court reporters make too much money." Which really meant: *You make more money than I do.* She didn't get it. She had a job to do. I had a business to run. It was supposed to be a collaboration built on teamwork.

What's worse, the EEOC Compliance Director at the time was also Black—and out of compliance. She refused to allow me to earn the $8,000–$10,000 I was due for four- and five-day hearings when judges flew in from D.C., instead, giving the work to my colleagues who were White contractors. She was disturbed by my relevance. I was the point person the agency had specifically sought out to meet their diversity goals, then called set-asides. My business had been selected after several small business incubator meetings. But this new director didn't bother to ask how the contract was supposed to flow—she just terminated it.

That was another defining moment for me. These were Blacks plagued by self-hate—perhaps the ugliest form of hatred. They couldn't stand to see me succeed. And money was the excuse she used to terminate my business, not job performance. That was the hardest thing to accept.

We see this happening every day in the workplace, the arena most vital to our survival. A year or so later, the contract went out for bid again—and the same EEOC Director sent me a copy to rebid. Just like before, I refused. Whatever problems she now had to overcome after unjustly terminating my contract were hers to solve. I launched out into the deep and kept moving forward.

We can only blame ourselves for the condition of our hearts when we watch young Black graduates enter the workplace and try to destroy the trailblazers who look just like them. It's a kind of self-destruction that resembles genocide. Intoxicated on power. We don't support each other's businesses—we sabotage, slander, and even rob them.

Someone had to blaze the trail that our young people now walk through so freely. But what I see is a willingness to overthrow one another with no second thought. They're offended by your success. Conditioned to sabotage. Desperate for relevance. Removed from the legacy of the 1950s and '60s Civil Rights Movement, they've convinced themselves racism is over. Wow.

They don't realize we're always under observation— always surveying or being surveyed. We were taught that if we treat people the way we want to be treated, everything would fall into place, but that's not always true. The truth is, Blacks are turning on Blacks.

What's more foreboding is the fact that nothing is ever said about it—it's swept under the rug. Everyone has a motive and intent behind their embrace of you—or their lack thereof. Often, that motive is driven by a need to assert control or identity, but it ultimately determines whether they will respect you. It's better known as abuse of power. Likewise, if they feel they can't manipulate you, you're labeled *"difficult,"* when in truth, *they're* the ones who are difficult, trying to make you abort your vision. Whether driven by ignorance or a lack of wisdom, their behavior often stems from an evil intent. On the other hand, if they sense fear or weakness in you, then you become prey for the predator.

No one ever warns you about the unpleasant people who thrive on being unpleasant, or the deceivers lying in wait, or the capitalists scheming to run a scam that will set you back financially. I don't know whether it would've been better to be forewarned about what's really out there in the "real world"—a world you'll have to face regardless. At some point, you either fight or retreat.

Now that I've lived this long, I understand how people end up homeless. They were simply ill-prepared for life's journey. They were sold a dream—told that life would be a bed of roses, but now they're sleeping on pillows of thorns and thistles. There's a harsh reality to being thrown into life unprepared. It feels like being pushed off a cliff and expected to fly—only to realize the world never wanted to see you fly in the first place. They never meant it when they told you to get a good education and make something of yourself.

Then, after you graduate from college, you find you can't get a job because everything is privatized. You learn that racism operates through "at-will" hire employment laws—they don't have to hire you. The jobs are for the entitled White males and females of this country. And now you're burdened with student loans, racism, discrimination, and confusion. What a distressing place to find oneself. Welcome to the real world!

Young people, driven by desperation, are forced to push out older or seasoned employees—elders who've paid their dues. Age discrimination is real. Instead of being appreciated, they're cast aside for not being "up-to-date."

Society claims it wants you to be a productive member, but the same society that cheered for you in college becomes your wrecking crew once you graduate. Especially if you're an independent thinker. You begin to see that some sectors are using the job market as a political stomping ground. If you've ever been fired through at-will policies, you know exactly what I'm talking about.

That's why one of my greatest achievements was becoming an entrepreneur. As a business owner, I watched people lose jobs due to layoffs, RIFs, job freezes, downsizing, rightsizing—whatever name they gave it. It's still termination.

It's eye-opening—how society builds you up just to tear you down when you don't share its values or political opinions. It will undermine your efforts just to maintain control over the job market and political agenda, offering little to no support when you're pushed out due to racism and discrimination. This is often the moment when young adults decide their political affiliation—it was for me. Losing a major job or contract forces you to take a stand.

Why weren't we warned about the condition of the human heart? Everybody's "zooming" one another—and I don't mean the online platform. And would we have even listened if someone had warned us?

As young adults, we think we've got it all figured out—get a good education, go to church, work hard, and everything will work out, but that's not always how it goes. That's when life gets real. Culture shock is the only way to describe what's happening in the 21st-century workplace.

There's little authenticity left. And when you do find it, someone with money often steals the idea, plagiarizes it, and passes it off as their own—stripping away the original intent and twisting the message until it loses its power. They push a false narrative just to make themselves look good.

These plagiarizers rarely grasp the full vision. They latch onto step one of an idea but leave everyone else in the dark about steps two and three. That's where we keep losing ground—while the world keeps kicking our butts.

As a young adult, I was never taught the dangers of capitalism or warned about the ruthlessness of people who don't want you to succeed—and will hurt or even destroy you to cover up their actions.

Instead of acknowledging the anointing or purpose on someone else's life, we now see schemers, liars, and false prophets running scared—afraid to open the door for true worship and discipleship. They can't stand the thought of being exposed.

But here's the thing about truth—it's like cream; it rises to the top.

People are perishing for lack of knowledge. If the man or woman of God refuses to spend time in the Word, the people get a bifurcated gospel—one with no substance. The church falls away, not because people aren't hungry, but because leaders refuse to rightly divide the Word. The Bible is clear: "Study to show yourself approved." But we keep missing the mark—and we all know that missing the mark is sin. And sin lies at the door.

Nowadays, if you have a bright idea, you'd better keep it to yourself until you can bring it to fruition. I refuse to share any more bright ideas with anyone before their time, as I've had two books plagiarized within religious circles and sermons preached directly quoting from the books—without the power source behind the words— simply because someone wished they had come up with the message or idea themselves.

I was given a vision to start the first Black Gospel talk show and called it *Just Churchin'*. At the time, I was at the wrong church. The preacher shared my idea with someone he knew who had the money and means to put it into motion. As I watched the show—under a different title—it didn't bode well for that pastor either, because he wasn't anointed, and the message came from a worldly perspective. It tanked. I learned a vital life lesson: never cast your pearls before swine.

Not to mention, approximately twelve years ago, I was a forerunner in broadcasting the message of finding one's identity in Christ—a message that quickly caught fire. A well-known pastor and preacher-ette began plagiarizing the concept of "Identity in Christ" as a viable answer to many of Christendom's problems. I've learned that when God gives you something to say and someone else steals it, at least it has been said. It was never about you anyway, but about God.

A friend of mine, Ernie, once said, "Imitation is the sincerest form of flattery." So I've learned not to take it personally, but rather to accept their plagiarism as flattery—even when they don't call my name. It's not about whether your name gets called. It's all about Jesus Christ and Him crucified. I came to understand that I was simply an instrument being used by Almighty God to help pave the way for the exponential growth of the church and the knowledge of the Word.

It's really not hard to spot the modern-day plagiarists—they're the ones gifted at blending politics with religion, many of whom are not studying or living God's Word themselves. For them, it's all about public persona and appearances rather than the indwelling presence of the Holy Spirit. In many churches today, you can feel a nightclub effect—they just have a sign out front calling it a church. I call it modern-day paganism. It's a type of Canaan land, a type of Sodom and Gomorrah—a virtual free-fall approach to greasy grace. They'll tell you that you can live any kind of way and still get to heaven.

THE POLITICS OF RELIGION

PART 1

The politics of religion tells me I can steal, kill, and destroy my fellow disciples' God-given ideas and concepts in order to sell CDs, cassettes, and videotapes—just to make money in the religious arena. But that's not something supported by the Word of God at all. This is the ultimate betrayal of God's Word. Not only were we commanded to esteem one another more highly than ourselves, but instead, we see that principle being completely reversed. There is no reciprocity. The thief just continues to steal, kill, and destroy. *You esteem me!* I don't have to esteem you. There are no checks, no balances whatsoever.

Instead of esteeming one another more highly, we oppress, suppress, and depress them. We place them into bondage, abort their birthing process—cut them off at the birthing stool. We have a problem with the phrase "more highly than ourselves," which implies there's some self-righteousness there. We were instructed to make disciples, to reproduce disciples, but instead, we malign the gifts and talents, the acquired skill sets, and seek to abort the messenger and the gifts God has placed in someone other than ourselves.

I've witnessed this spirit among false teachers and preachers, among musicians and singers who have turned the church into a gospel music enterprise rather than a place of worship. This is why so many of the gifted churchgoers went out into the world in the first place—seeking recognition from the world rather than from God.

We're grieved at the very thought of God using someone other than ourselves. To esteem you higher than me? Unimaginable. I can't fathom someone being "higher" than me, so I choose not to accept you, let alone esteem you. And to those of you standing just outside the gate— know that it's confirmation you are indeed a child of God. *They esteemed Him not.* Just as they did unto Jesus, so too they will do to you. On their part, sin lies at the door—just like Cain with Abel. Choosing to sin against your brother or sister because you've decided not to give God your best leads you to minimize the accomplishments and gifts of others. Then you'll solicit others like yourself to lie against the truth. Cain's act against Abel was one of premeditated intent. If someone is going to be higher, that must mean someone else has to be lower.

And what's worse are the subtle but pernicious advances from the pastor as you exit the church. He's standing there, and as you reach to shake his hand, he blurts out, "When are we gonna get together?" You shake his hand halfheartedly, then rush to exit while processing his inappropriate request. Based on what just happened, you know you won't be singing lead songs at his church. It's like a spiritual tug-of-war—when you do sing lead, everybody wants to "get with you." And if you're not loyal to the unspoken pact, you don't sing lead at all. It's disgusting. It's abominable behavior.

Unfortunately, musicians and singers—choir members—are often the worst at taking each other out. We see recording artists who've bolted the door shut on others they know without a doubt are anointed, holding back the gifts and talents of God in unrighteousness just to stay out front. What happened is this: When the pastor asked them after church when they'd "get together," they didn't hesitate to say, "Much obliged." Now their relationship has tanked, and everyone else in the choir is being held hostage. It's not hard to figure out. I simply refuse to play the game.

At the rate we're going, we'll all remain limited, uneducated, and lacking in entrepreneurial ability until some of our leaders grow up and allow successful entrepreneurs to share their journeys—rather than competing with their own members. Many leaders are limited, trying to speak about places they've never even traveled. I've seen church members with great vision and ideas to start businesses, only to have their dream hijacked by the pastor and his wife, who then open up a consignment shop or chicken wing franchise. But as quickly as it was stolen and opened, it tanked. The business was a total failure.

There's nothing worse than a word that's been twisted—it can cause many to stumble. Granted, there's a difference between imparting a word of knowledge to help others grow, and standing in the pulpit teaching with a spirit of envy and jealousy—killing the church, killing dreams—because you didn't go to college, or because you can't sing. This type of religion is plastic, fake, hypocritical. It represents the spirit of Cain—that wicked one.

Because when you're listening for the voice of God in a message or sermon, if the words are stolen, it always leaves a void—a longing for truth. There's nothing worse than a lackluster or powerless word, an inapplicable word that doesn't quite connect with your spirit. There's a sense of emptiness in your soul telling you the word has fallen flat. You can't apply it to your life. You have nothing to hold onto next week when trouble comes knocking. Words that are devoid of meaning and direction—like arrows shot into the air, lost among the trees in a forest; no one knows where they land.

Yes, we continue to lose ground—over and over—because of the dominant male ego, which, if unchecked, can derail not only the church, but your life.

We need a 21st-century word for a 21st-century workplace. However, it's best to remain candidly cautious as we go through life, because in all probability, we'll find that we're not here to stay. We're trekking through a temporal world. What feels like a lifetime to us is really only a season. We're not here to stay. We live among family and loved ones, and yet our ancestors who have gone on before us have passed into another time and space. So, it's best not to take too much too seriously. It's best not to get caught up in houses, cars, land, clothes—stuff.

Even more so, it's best not to get caught up in what others think or say about you. I've found this to be one of the greatest lessons in life. Don't let others define who you are, who they think you should be, or how they think you should act. Many of them don't even know who *they* are— and they're never going to admit that. Healthy-minded people don't target others.

As you go through life, you'll be knocked down many times. You'll get the wind knocked out of you—trust me on that—more times than you can imagine. Life's circumstances will hit hard, but it's all about how you get back up again, and again, and again. It's all by faith. And I'm not talking about falling because of some wrongdoing that brings punishment on yourself, but simply falling because that's the way life has always been since the beginning of time.

Since the fall of Adam and Eve, humanity has been in a perpetual state of falling; but each time you fall, there's something to be learned—something that causes you to grow spiritually and begin making better choices. In my case, in 1979, I was the only Black student in my class to graduate in my field. I considered myself a trailblazer, like Hattie McDaniel.

It's like going to look for a job, spending forty-five minutes filling out the application, only to be told they're not hiring. You smile and move on to your next destination. Then it happens again. You fill out another application, and they're not hiring either. It begins to feel like the wind is being knocked right out of you.

On the way back to your car, you feel like you're hyperventilating. You can hardly breathe, and by the time this happens five or six more times in a single day, you begin to understand what it truly means to have the wind knocked out of you. Still, you encourage yourself at the end of each day, only to get back up the next morning and start the process all over again.

Today, we've transitioned into a digital era where you can apply for jobs from your home computer or even right at the store. But the emotional toll remains. With a heavy heart, you encourage yourself in a time and space designed either to break your spirit or to mold you into a spiritual giant. That's what true faith is.

Even with all the traps set along life's journey—many of which you didn't set yourself—you still have to put on a "happy face" and go out looking for any job that can help put food on the table and clothes on your back.

No one ever tells you how to deal with having the wind knocked out of you on the tough streets of life. Maybe someone failed to share their story. Maybe they fainted somewhere along their journey. Maybe they left you to figure it out for yourself. Or maybe they were so overwhelmed by their own trials that they forgot how to stop and enjoy life.

But that's what you *must* do—stop and enjoy life. Even in the midst of bad times, you have to intentionally seek out the good; that takes effort. The good can be easy to overlook, but I've learned to stop and smell the roses. We must not let life pass us by.

Even when you've played by the rules and done everything the right way, life can still be most challenging. That's when you're most tempted to throw in the towel. Life's winds can blow so fiercely that your hopes and dreams get swept away in a whirlwind. We're literally seeing this today—lives being swept away by hurricanes and tornadoes. Could it be that God is trying to get our attention?

Everything some people have worked for becomes one big pile of rubbish—twisted and mangled into debris. There's a message in there somewhere.

We've built our lives on material things—cars, homes, clothes—and the woke generation would add tattoos, eccentric fake nails, and false eyelashes to the list. *Stuff.* And when that stuff is taken away, we're left to ask: Is this all there is to life? *Is this it?* As we look at what remains of our lives piled up in heaps of rubble and twisted metal, could it be that somewhere along the way we forgot to include God in our daily affairs?

71

Now, we're being forced to learn from disasters. If it's not an earthquake, it's a tornado—or lately, a tsunami. It's only when disaster strikes that we become humble, kind, and pliable, and that's only because we were forced into it. Life's disasters force us to take a long, hard look at ourselves and who we've become.

Take Hurricane Katrina, for example. Once homelessness becomes the only option, humility, compassion, and brotherly love quickly follow. Then—and only then—do we realize how fast it can all be taken away. Life can change in the blink of an eye. We take so much for granted.

We make gods out of our stuff. We make gods out of our families and loved ones. We even set ourselves apart based on who has the most stuff—who lives in the biggest house, drives the fanciest car, or attended the most prestigious college or university—only to discover, in times of disaster, that the things we've spent a lifetime accumulating weren't worth the struggle at all. We come to realize we are more vulnerable than we thought, and once our stuff is gone, we're left alone to deal with ourselves.

Just a month ago, we witnessed over 1,600 homes and structures burn to the ground in California wildfires. The Palisades community took a huge hit, along with the insurance industry, but this wasn't the first time we've seen devastating fires in California or the western states.

Hollywood raises our children, while the secular world joins forces to support one another's concepts and ideas. Our children mimic what they see on television—joining gangs, acting out scripted behaviors in real life—and we wonder why guns have become so popular among the youth. Meanwhile, Hollywood takes no responsibility for what it puts on our screens, as long as it makes money.

A formative mind is a terrible thing to waste. If it's not sex, it's drugs. If it's not drugs, it's violence. If it's not violence, it's politics. And if not politics, it's some overly delusional, psychotic, or psychopathic content—saturated with extreme animation to the point that we can't tell whether it's real or artificial intelligence. We've resorted to high animation, and it's so over-the-top that movies have lost their humanistic qualities. I personally preferred the days when people really knew how to act—without the need for digital overkill.

Even with our advancements, technology is out of control. Today, if you don't know how to fill out an application online, you won't get a job. We're quickly becoming a paperless society. Technology moves so fast that no one group or segment can keep up—especially the elderly. Enter your password here, your username there, your ID somewhere else... and don't forget to write it all down so you don't forget where it is! These days, we have ten or more passwords just for work, banking, and personal accounts. If you're like me, your office is scattered with legal pads full of scribbled notes, passwords, and login info.

Keeping up with technology has placed an enormous burden on us all, and no one is communicating on the same level. By the time you learn one system, another one hits the market—and yours is already outdated. Since going digital, even some of the so-called "tech experts" aren't sure the gadgets do what they're supposed to do. Remember the evolution of the computer? First the 286, then 386, 486, Pentium 1, Pentium 2, Pentium 3... then Terabyte 1, 2, 3, and so on. Maybe we've finally reached a pause—and that might be a good thing.

Take texting, for instance. It's monopolized the way we communicate, and people are literally dying in the name of technology—trying to prove they're some sort of superhuman multitasker while driving. It's dangerous, it's irresponsible, and yet no one seems to care. These products are rushed to market as a fast way to make money, then discontinued without warning.

If you own a small business that's low on capital, trying to keep up with technology can put you out of business. Don't let high tech become more important than your clients' needs. Courteous, prompt, and dependable service matters more. The clients who can afford the newest tech are few, and they're often the ones demanding that everyone else keep up with them.

My small business experienced its own peaks and valleys. It ebbed and flowed. When profits were up, things were good. When profits went down, it was extremely slow—like most small businesses. It was like riding a high surf at noon, only to have the wave fizzle by the evening tide. So when I needed to upgrade my technology, I had to spend money I didn't have. Instead of going high-tech during slow seasons, I focused on providing dependable, quality service. That allowed me to compete, even with limited resources. I bought new software and equipment only when it made sense for my business plan—often waiting for sales.

I couldn't afford to go high-tech, especially due to the racism and discrimination that hindered my ability to make money in the workplace. The bright side? I received very few complaints throughout the year. But as a Black small business owner, my progress was often blocked by the "gatekeepers."

When working with the state, those gatekeepers were the contract compliance officers, purchasing departments, and administrators who funneled work to my White colleagues. On one occasion, a contract compliance officer even refused to honor my mileage reimbursement on an invoice. I had driven over 300 miles for an assignment. That officer was eventually walked off the job—given ten minutes to pack his things and leave the building.

Workplace harassment and intimidation are real. You have to stay vigilant in how you deal with gatekeepers who try to force you out for any minor infraction—most of which they create themselves. They especially hate seeing you make more money than them. In my case, that officer was terminated on the spot—and rightfully so.

At the time, the state was making efforts to work with competent small, woman-owned DEI businesses. Being the only Black woman in my field made my business a rare commodity.

Nevertheless, I pressed forward as a trailblazer into uncharted territory. There still hadn't been a Black Court Reporter in my hometown in nearly 25 years, so the path was lonely and often filled with pressure and stress that the average 9-to-5 employee would never experience.

No one tells you that if you're Black, you'll likely be in a constant state of flux in the workplace for most of your career. That's something someone should have shared after the Civil Rights Movement—that if you dare to dream big and possess intellectual knowledge and expertise in a particular field or discipline, you will be misunderstood. Count on it. You're constantly challenged—sometimes openly—by agency cronies, and even by witnesses during depositions. I was told repeatedly, "They're not gonna let you do that." "No Black is smart enough to do that." "It's never been done before." I never really understood what they meant by that.

Forty years ago, it was unheard of—a Black Court Reporter in an all-White judicial system. In fact, I actually integrated the judicial system after the Civil Rights Movement. What's ironic is, that I did it by sheer happenstance, almost like I stumbled into it. I never gave much thought to being the only Black person in the courtroom or what people would think of me. My motivation was pure—just a desire to achieve my goals and dreams. Never once did I think, "I'm going to integrate the judicial system." But it happened.

And so, time after time, you must learn how to push past the challenges. Never give up. Never give in.

Here we are, over forty years later, and the doors that were once difficult to open have now opened for our own Black youth and young adult college graduates—many of whom know nothing of the struggles of the '60s, or of Diversity, Equity, and Inclusion initiatives, Set-Asides, or even Affirmative Action or EEOC efforts. Now, they find themselves in well-paying jobs right out of college, all across this nation. Yet some refuse to launch out at all. What's uncanny is the fact that many have become part of the problem. When they see other successful Black, woman-owned businesses that have made it through the tough times in the workplace, they will often attempt to erase the very path that was paved—cut down and plowed through by those who came before us eighty or so years ago. Some will even terminate your contract themselves, simply because they now have the power to do so.

I've had Black attorneys—with just one year of legal experience, fresh out of an HBCU—do exactly that. You've been with the agency for fifteen successful years, and they come in and take on the persona of the hater simply because you are successful, and because they now hold power, they subvert your destiny. It's a disturbing and disheartening development among Blacks in the workplace. They don't realize that the very door they just walked through was opened by someone else who fought for it—someone who endured vicious dogs, billy clubs, metal pipes, and bombs to make that path possible. It's unfathomable conduct, especially from graduates of HBCUs.

Since the recession of 2008, it seems the workplace has shifted into survival mode. The housing bubble had burst, leaving many with upside-down mortgages. Now more than ever, the ability to discern someone's energy—whether good or bad—is critical. We each have a choice: to be a positive force of encouragement or a formidable force of destruction in someone else's life.

No one ever warns you about the games people play in the workplace—not even a hint of the dissension that lies ahead.

In the job market, there are all kinds of power seekers—Black and White—just waiting to take you out. They don't care how much knowledge or education you've acquired, or whether you're called Doctor or Professor. Intoxicated with power, they're just itching to exercise their authority over you. That's exactly what happened in my case. The powers that be couldn't handle the fact that I had become a successful Black businesswoman and decided to change my destiny after thirty-five years of struggle.

THE POLITICS OF RELIGION

PART 2

U nfortunately, we must be encouraged and know that there's going to come a time when you have to take a stand—and often, that's within the judicial system. It goes without saying. If somehow God delivers Goliath into your hands, make sure you cut his head off—David did. We have to learn to fight back, even if it's among our own Black peers. And if someone had told you at the outset that you'd have to fight at all in the workplace, you would've labeled them paranoid or delusional.

We've been taught to love the unlovable, and that's all well and good, but I say: when you're losing your home, your car, and the ability to survive, it's imperative that you develop your fighting instincts in the workplace rather than remain passive-aggressive. Passive-aggressive people often get squashed—and there's nothing like a good squashing to make you get back up and fight. Just remember to do it legally.

The workplace is not a playground, nor is it a proverbial sandbox or dating site—but because a lot of small-thinking people have made it those things, you have to develop life skills, survival skills, the skill of being as wise as a serpent but harmless as a dove, as you go about meticulously documenting each and every event that has the potential to disrupt your business affairs. It's the only way you're going to survive in the 21st-century workplace.

However, of late, we've seen workplace harassment taken to its highest level of torment. The pain is so overwhelming and excruciating that professors and teachers are losing their minds—and sometimes their lives—due to non-renewal of contracts or denial of tenure. They become the judge, jury, and executioner. What a tragedy. Not to mention teachers choosing to date their students rather than teach them—some even bearing children with their students. The games people play in the workplace are becoming more and more deadly. What an example to set for students. It can happen to anyone. In my case, the judge watched her secretary take a swing at me from the floor, then decided to terminate my contract with absolutely no mention of the workplace violence committed by her secretary. Then to go on and say that I became angry – I sure did. All of this was because I sat in an elevated seat in court and she did not, and the secretary's friend eventually ended up with what used to be my hard earned promotion.

We've witnessed Columbine and Virginia Tech, but never did we think there would come a day when we'd see a professor in a severe mental health crisis, similar to that of the students he teaches, break down due to workplace harassment and denial of tenure. The inability to cope in hostile environments is real, yet the topic continues to go unaddressed—bullying in the workplace. There is no place for workplace violence. We'd like to assume that adults know how to behave, but that assumption has become a travesty in this nation. It's totally unacceptable.

There has to be another way to address the people we perceive to have injured us. It's true that batters batter and bullies bully, and that those who have been deprived often deprive others. These dynamics stem from unresolved childhood issues and lie dormant until they appear at your door. Even those who assault others violently at work often want what you have—without merit, without earning it, without paying the price it took you to accomplish your goals. So they tear up the workplace with tantrums and tears, driven by envy, like Cain, who destroyed his brother because his own works were evil, and his brother's were righteous. It's a spiritual dilemma.

That's why I say: document, document, document!

Documentation is better than jail time. A cursory review of those who chose violence bears that out—it's better to fight it out in court than in the workplace. It's okay to call out bad behavior through the HR department. That's what the judicial system is for. Instead of a classroom, some now have a jail cell to contend with—a place to rehearse their sinful behavior for a lifetime.

81

Violence in the workplace is a spiritual issue, not just a carnal one. Taking matters into your own hands is not the answer. In retrospect, it all had been a plan to force me out of the promotion, and give the position to the judge's secretary's friend. I don't know if she's still there, but it was all done because of nepotism, and nobody bothered to check it out. It wasn't a 'Who Dun It', it was more of a 'Who You Know."

It was not the secretary's call to make. I was constantly harassed and assaulted openly even when the judge was present; the judge did absolutely nothing about it. There was obviously a conflict of interest, and the secretary's friend had worked in the DA's office for over 25 years, and had given up the field of Court Reporting. She'd never earned the position, and quite frankly, had abandoned the field altogether, stating to me, "Court Reporting is the most racist thing I've ever done." Yet, they took it from me and gave it to her.

There was never any mention of workplace violence or zero tolerance. It was swept under the rug, as though the judge enjoyed the drama. In fact, she was all in as they sabotaged my career. I was being bullied by five haters in the workplace. I can only say: I was ganged up on by five women trying to force me out of a six-figure contract so the judge's assistant could hand the position to her friend— who had a clear conflict of interest and should never have been given the role in the first place.

All of this happened over a period of six years, but I kept getting up, going about the business of fulfilling my contract's obligations and scope of work under extreme duress. Still, I kept picking myself up, brushing myself off, and doing a great job. I believe I had only one complaint in six years, and it was about a page number.

The fact that I had been appointed by the Governor in 2014 to a promotion covering four criminal courts in an all-White district—being the first Black person to ever work in any of these courts—and that I was working with the Governor's Office of Diversity Business Development, a DEI program for small business development, had been a great support.

Since COVID and the dismantling of all DEI initiatives in our state, this program has likely been discontinued as well. The following events expose the cover-up that led to the dismantling of the DEI initiative in the state.

The next event changed everything for me: I found out that I had to have a hysterectomy. All of my medical records were accessed without my knowledge or consent—an invasion of privacy, and a felony HIPAA violation. No warrant was issued, and I wasn't given any due process rights. If I was under investigation, I was never informed. All I remember is my doctor telling me that I needed to find another job. It didn't dawn on me what he meant until the day of surgery. I had 45 benign tumors removed in a total hysterectomy.

Subsequent to the surgery, I was almost killed by the anesthesiologist, who I believe was sent there by the judge I worked for—all to remove me from the position I had earned by merit, and to give my job to the judge's assistant's friend. There were several co-conspirators who will remain unnamed, but they participated in helping the judge devise the entire scheme.

After surgery, I was physically assaulted with an iron pipe approximately 15 inches long. The anesthesiologist began pounding on my left mid-thigh until I began to spasm and lose consciousness—this was attempted murder. I flatlined. The most terrifying part was that my body had been numbed. I could not sit up, walk, or run—I was completely helpless.

As of this writing in 2025, I have yet to find an attorney willing to hold this group of thugs accountable, although I have spoken to numerous media outlets about the hate crime. I actually began to spasm on the OR table and flatlined. It was a horrific nightmare that continues to be covered up in order to protect those involved. The Rule of Law was violated—and so was the Hippocratic Oath: *Do no harm.* My hope is that by sharing this in a book, the truth will come to light and someone will be held accountable. There is no statute of limitations on attempted murder.

To add to this tragedy, it's been nearly five years since it happened, and my business has lost $500,000 due to the termination of a 28-year contract with the Tennessee

Supreme Court. I was terminated because of my race, and a hate crime was committed.

This was a violation of my 14th Amendment rights, a violation of my 4th Amendment protection against illegal search and seizure, a HIPAA violation (a felony), an attempted murder, and a conspiracy.

When people look over and see their brothers and sisters doing something meaningful and noteworthy—something that earns them a promotion—and then try to have them killed or defame them based on carnal perception, that's how workplace shootings and mass killings happen. Cain killed Abel for a similar reason—because his own works were evil and his brother's were righteous. Promotion comes from God. Cain was cursed by God until he returned to the dust from which he came.

Look, people, this same dynamic is still happening today, but you must see it with spiritual eyes—not carnal ones. The carnal mind cannot receive the things of God. Satan has blinded their minds so they cannot see the spiritual realities that surround us, leading them to steal, kill, and destroy their brothers and sisters. Those who are spiritual are accepted by God. Those who are carnal cannot come to the knowledge of the truth.

Still, you must put the offender on notice. Let them know: if their behavior continues, you will take out a warrant and have them arrested for assault and battery. If they keep harassing you without cause, they will find themselves standing before a judge—handcuffed—trying to explain why they kept hitting or bumping into you at work. I've documented numerous cases of workplace assault when working with the Department of Personnel, and Human Resources over six years.

About ten years ago, I handled a case where a young woman kept bumping into her boss in the hallway—all because of jealousy. It eventually reached HR and led to a formal hearing. Hold people accountable for their conduct. Don't hide it. If necessary, call out their psychiatric or mental health condition. It was likely something she'd done before in her family—bullying behavior that she thought was acceptable in the workplace. Fortunately, she didn't bring a gun to work and shoot her boss. That's why I say: *Don't let it pass.* See something, say something.

It could've gone another way. They could've fought, and someone could've ended up dead.

Truly, if someone is crazy enough to harass you or punch you, you have the right to take action—even if that means getting them help from behind bars. What they think is acceptable behavior is criminal. Sometimes people don't get help until they're incarcerated—until they've had time to reflect. That's why it's called the Department of Corrections.

No one has the right to punch, torture, or brutalize you in the workplace—just because they can. Often, they're sick, and their actions are speaking for them. They're just waiting for someone to stop the locomotive before it crashes into someone's life or career. They are actually screaming for help—crying, *Stop me!* Many of them can't even explain their own behavior. It's just plain devilish.

Remember, no one is above the law. Many times, it's easy to become overtaken by the pain of an action, which can cause you to react without thinking—fight or flight, kill or be killed. But there's a thin line that divides the sane from the insane. Just don't internalize the pain to the point that you relive the event so intensely that you become a self-made vigilante. It's tempting—and easy to do. But there is a difference between revenge and justice.

Some offenders see nothing wrong with their behavior at all and will resent your suggestion that they've done anything requiring forgiveness. They don't want to be forgiven, because they have no intention of acknowledging their harassment or attacks against you in the workplace—let alone changing their behavior. To them, their harassment is just a tool—a way to control the situation, assert superiority, and either run you off the job or out of the church. I call it the desecration of the Rule of Law.

They blame you for their deficiencies and shortcomings. In many instances, they are threatened by you. You possess a spirit of excellence—they do not. Ultimately, their actions reflect how they feel about themselves. For them, it's always someone else's fault. They can't handle your uniqueness, your authenticity, your commitment to righteousness, so they sit back and compare themselves to others—and you likely make them feel like a counterfeit, as evidenced by how they treat you.

It's always someone else's fault that their marriage is in shambles, that their spouse is cheating—or that they are cheating. They drag you into their pain and project their inner turmoil onto you. So they come after your peace of mind, your confidence, your reputation. And when you're dragged into someone else's unresolved pain, there's a good chance they're living a life filled with confusion and suffering.

THE POLITICS OF RELIGION

PART 3

I'll never forget the day I joined a church because I sang in the choir with many of its members—which turned out to be the worst decision I could have ever made. By the time I attended my first church meeting, they were asking the pastor to step down—wow! I thought, *What have I gotten myself into?* Apparently, he had committed some kind of infraction during a church outing at a swimming pool with a woman. I began devising an exit strategy immediately.

Only later did I find out that he and his first wife were getting a divorce so he could be with another woman from a different church—the red flags flew ferociously. When his new girlfriend arrived to take the first wife's place, she was bitter toward every woman in the church she thought had been involved with him. Because I was successful, owned my own business, and had an education and blessings she didn't possess, I became a target of her jealousy.

During a church outing where we were singing in the choir stand at an outdoor event, she suddenly rushed the choir stand and got in my face for absolutely no reason, completely unprovoked—as if to say, *I got you!* The Holy Spirit spoke to me immediately: *You've been injured, but it's not unto death.* She did this in front of the entire choir, without warning or explanation.

When I got home from the outing, I got out of the car, locked the door, and walked toward the steps—only to turn around and notice a huge dent in the front panel on the driver's side of my Mercedes-Benz. Whoever hit it, hit it hard—with force and intention. I didn't understand the motive behind the violence, but I recognized immediately that this was what the Holy Spirit had revealed to me earlier in the choir stand. I connected the two incidents instantly and knew either she or one of her two brothers had punched the car. However, neither of her brothers were at the outing—only she and the pastor were present. He had walked up behind her at the event, arms outstretched, trying to remove her from my face just before she turned around.

This led me to believe she had used the pastor—her husband—to hurt me in some way. Which meant he was sick too. That dent in my car became a symbol of her pain and her desire to lash out, possibly because she felt threatened by my presence in the congregation. Shortly after, I left the church. I could have taken them to court, but I knew it would be a waste of time and money. I trusted God to handle it. All because of jealousy.

It's okay to leave a toxic environment—whether it's in the workplace, at church, or elsewhere—especially when value systems don't align. What kind of pastor would damage a church member's car? He had to be emotionally or spiritually unwell. And to this day, their church membership has dwindled down to almost nothing. He now relies on outside speaking engagements just to keep the church afloat.

These are the types of churches that resemble cults. I wouldn't recommend anyone attend a place so full of confusion and conflict, where God's Word is neither preached nor lived—from a pure heart.

THE BATTLEGROUND

PART 1

After thirty-five years in business—thirty-five years of providing prompt and proficient service—it's devastating to have someone intentionally give your contract to a friend during a recession. Now, you're about to lose your home, your car, and your career, all because of nepotism and racism. Because you're Black. Because Blacks aren't supposed to dream big. And it's not even that the work went away—it's that the wall of racism was shoved right in your face. What an awful way to say "thank you" for doing a great job these past six years.

And let's not forget the fact that you've been threatened with being lynched—for what? I'd say the time to speak up is now. If you don't, they might make good on that threat, and no one will ever know it happened. I was told by one of the court clerks in the breakroom, "We'll string you up, and take your body parts and spread them across the mountain, and nobody will ever find them." I was flabbergasted. She was talking about dismemberment. Really?

And if you do tell, maybe—just maybe—they'll come to their senses and realize they've made a terroristic threat, which is a hate crime in America, punishable by imprisonment or life. No matter how you look at it, for your own safety and well-being, you have a duty and an obligation to report workplace harassment, violence, and intimidation. And all this drama—for what? For being a successful Black small business owner in America.

Flashback! This takes me back to 1980, just after I finished court reporting school and accepted a position in criminal court in another state. I had weighed the pros and cons. Tired of dead-end jobs at the local power distributor— always downsizing, right-sizing, sending out RIF notices—I decided to accept the court reporting position. The position offered about $8,000 more per year, and it seemed like a step in the right direction. They promised benefits, overtime pay, and reimbursement for moving expenses – but it was all a lie.

I packed up a U-Haul and made the move. I got a check for $300.00 for moving expenses and found an apartment outside the city. At first, things went smoothly. But overtime pay? That became a major issue. I was told I'd be paid for anything after 4:30 p.m., yet I often sat in court until 8:00 or 9:00 at night several days a week, with no extra compensation. They refused to pay overtime. After driving home late at night, I'd spend another two or three hours dictating notes for the typist, then try to get some sleep before starting all over the next day—still with no overtime pay. I was in a rut.

At the time, there were only five Black court reporters in the city. Most worked at that same criminal court, except for two. The courthouse itself was an old dilapidated building, and at night vagrants would sleep in the stairwells, urinate there, and leave before court began. You'd arrive in the morning having to step over blankets and puddles of urine, and try not to choke from the stench as you climbed the stairs. This wasn't what I had envisioned.

Still, no overtime, no benefits. Then, two other reporters who had worked there before me started sharing horror stories about our boss. Apparently, none of them had benefits either. I began asking the attorneys for overtime pay or else I would leave at 4:30. I refused to work for free. That stirred up conflict. I learned this had been going on before I even arrived.

Here I was—house full of furniture, surrounded by disgruntled employees. I'd been tricked and scammed. They had also told me that the reporters rotated between courtrooms, but no one was ever willing to rotate. I didn't mind at first because my judge had a strong, clear voice, and I could catch every word.

Then things took a turn. The Mayor appointed a Black female judge—her first time in the role—and she didn't know her job. What's worse, she whispered. I couldn't tell if it was intentional gaslighting or an attempt to cover up the fact that she didn't know her job. About four or five months in, she began lashing out, using me as her scapegoat whenever she felt pressured. She'd freak out whenever I asked her to speak louder.

Tensions flared. With other reporters refusing to rotate, I was stuck with her. One day during a break, we were in the breakroom. I took a short restroom break and came back to sit down. The judge told me, "Be quiet." I thought, *There's no one else here to talk to anyway.* Then a public defender walked in and said hello. I replied, "Hello." I glanced down at her shoes and said, "Cute shoes."

All at once, the judge yelled at the top of her lungs, "God damn it! I said shut up!" It was a knee-jerk reaction—I stood up and yelled back, "F*** you!" The public defender was stunned. Speechless.

From that moment on, I refused to let her use me as a punching bag when she was stressed. I reported her to the Chief Judge. Things only got worse from there. She became obsessed with revenge, targeting me for filing the report. No male judge had ever "cussed" me like that—and I use the word "cussed" because that's exactly how she spoke, like she was from the streets. No one—not my mother, father, or grandmother—had ever spoken to me that way. I wasn't going to tolerate it.

We continued working in that toxic environment for another month. Then she instructed the court deputy to slam a wrought iron door on me. It was heavy and locked with a skeleton key. That was the final straw. I cried in the restroom. Every time I asked her to speak up, she shouted, "No!"

Between the door incident, no overtime pay, refusal to rotate, lack of benefits, cussing, and yelling—I finally had enough. I got up and walked out of her courtroom. It was after 4:30, and I was done working for free.

The threat came quickly: "If you walk out of my courtroom again, I'll make sure you never work in any court again." All because I refused to work unpaid overtime. That wasn't what I agreed to when I accepted the position. I later learned there had been long standing disputes with the city about rates charged by our firm—something they never told me before I moved. I had been set up.

Looking back, the other court reporters were also disgruntled and wanted to stage a walkout. But I wasn't going to be assaulted or disrespected by a judge seeking revenge. I quit.

I walked away. Nothing was going as planned. I went on to seek other opportunities. I firmly believe—if you can't respect me as a valuable member of the team, then you need to find someone else to disrespect, but it won't be me.

This is where we're losing ground as Black people—turning back the clock to the pre-Civil Rights era—as we fight one another in the workplace, even with the doors of opportunity standing wide open for all of us to make a difference. She was the first DEI female at that time, and I was one of only three Black female court reporters in the city. Clearly, she had issues with me. One of her court deputies—a former pro-ball player who had been injured and was now working in court—had taken an interest in me, and that's when the stalking began. She wanted revenge.

I can honestly say I've been stalked by her for over forty years now. She makes it a point to find me and give a bad recommendation just to hinder my ability to work.

Within two weeks of quitting, I was hired at a new court reporting firm. I landed a huge hearing, and one day while working, two detectives walked into the agency and asked to see me. My boss came to get me and said they wanted to speak with me. I stepped into a small conference room, sat down at a table, and they laid out a photo array of several people. They asked if I recognized anyone. I looked through the photos but didn't recognize a single person. The detectives left.

However, because I had been questioned by detectives, my boss said, "We've never had anything like this happen at our firm," and I was asked to leave. I was officially terminated. Someone had sent those detectives there. The only person I had spoken to the week before—who knew I had a new position—was one of the court reporters back at the courthouse. She must have shared the information with the judge I had worked for, who was the only person with the power to stage a fake interview with detectives. I had been set up. It was an abuse of power. I wasn't her lover—I was her court reporter.

I was in the middle of a battleground, back to square one. I kept trying to untangle the web of deceit I found myself caught in since day one, now being stalked by a judge, trapped in a senseless set of circumstances that weren't panning out. I'd been misled by a desperate individual who needed help on his city contract and tricked me into thinking he had a position available—with benefits and overtime. None of it was true.

I went through at least two more agencies. Just as I was getting back on my feet, the judge would call and get me fired again. I called it what it was—**stalking**.

It got worse. I had a deposition on the northwest side of town, and after finishing, I stopped by Kroger to pick up some ribs for the long 4th of July holiday weekend. I was hit in the parking lot by a guy speeding through. My right foot was broken, and I suffered a crush injury to my toes. I had no idea what was going on. Could it have been a hit? I quickly dismissed the thought and was taken by ambulance to the hospital, where I stayed for 14 hours in the emergency room. They took x-rays and put my foot in a cast. Still, I couldn't figure out what was happening.

Then, at choir rehearsal, while at church, one of the male members—after seeing my cast—offered his take on what had happened. He believed it was intentional. He told me, "You were run down in a parking lot. That wasn't an accident." He believed it was an attempted murder. And the only person who had it in for me was the judge. As a judge, she probably felt she was above the law—that she could have me killed if she wanted. I had tried to brush it off as an accident, but after that conversation, I started to believe it was premeditated.

Writing this book is the only way I know to tell my side of the story.

I don't even see this as racism—it's a form of hatred that only the truly evil possess. A mental sickness born of jealousy, envy, and arrogance. You can't make this stuff up without premeditation. And to stalk someone you once attacked? That's a new level of depravity. You laid the groundwork. You set the tone. Now you're obsessed because of the damage you, yourself, caused.

Among Black people, there seems to be a kind of self-hate—a loathing that's hard to explain. I believe it stems from how they feel about themselves. Many don't want to see another Black person succeed, run a thriving business, or walk in the gifts they don't possess. In the workplace, we've become our own worst enemy.

It was clear to me that my life was in danger. I decided to return home and start my business with a fresh new approach—in a more positive environment, without all the workplace strife and dissension.

THE BATTLEGROUND

PART 2

Fast-forward to the 21st century, I'd say: wherever possible, record and document any and all ill-spoken words. Learn how to hold people accountable—while holding your own tongue. People need to be held responsible for their words and the tone in which they speak them in the workplace. Keep a daily diary—a running log of events as they transpire. Stay professional. I'm not suggesting that you become a doormat or allow yourself to be abused in a hostile work environment. Know that it's okay to defend yourself—especially when things become physical. Generally, when someone is threatening violence or even murder, that is a clear sign of aggression and mental derangement.

The most essential element is to ensure that **you're not the one** provoking the altercation, instigating conflict, or inciting confusion. Learn to walk away. Avoid harsh tones in tense workplace situations—it builds character and mental fortitude. Learn to smile, even when you feel anxious. Know there will be times, however, when you must speak up for yourself—especially when someone is provoking or threatening you, as in my case, taking a swing at you. Refuse to become fearful or agitated by hostile employees.

I remember once, while riding in the elevator, a judge said to me out of the blue, "They're gonna string you up, and I'm gonna be standing in the crowd watching!" Then he added, "Nobody's gonna want to see you coming!" I didn't understand. Was that his wish—not to see me coming? He said, "You come all the time." But it was my DEI contract with the state—I had to come regularly or be charged with non-performance. Hearings, jury trials, and labor relation arbitration sessions were a part of fulfilling my contractual duties. It seemed they had grown accustomed to an all-White courtroom. He didn't bite his tongue. I definitely broke new ground as the trailblazer I'd become—and the racism was quite apparent.

I remember joking with my college instructor about it. The simple fact that I was fulfilling my contractual obligations offended this judge. I was stunned by the audacity of his words—especially since I'd had no complaints in over six years. It was clear he believed I shouldn't be allowed to work in the field. In his mind, inclusion wasn't necessary; exclusivity was preferred. That's why DEI programs were created in the first place—to break through the exclusivity that kept competent Black professionals out of many career fields, especially small business ownership.

The fact that I was the first African-American to penetrate that glass ceiling made me a target of much hate speech and unwarranted criticism—from individuals who had never seen a Black court reporter before, let alone one who held over 15 contracts in a 35-year career. But to have someone look you in the face and say you're going to get lynched—it doesn't get more disgusting than that. And when you file a complaint, what I've seen happen is that **you**, the contractor, are removed—not the court sanctioned for unethical conduct. In other words, you're punished for their misconduct.

His statement was unprovoked. The fact that he described a lynching at all made it clear: he was a racist. He said he'd enjoy seeing me dangling from a tree. That nauseated me. This was a sitting judge, making inflammatory, hateful statements to an officer of the court—as if he were above the law. It took every ounce of courage to walk into the courtroom and proceed with the case. I knew I couldn't stop the hearing to step outside and cry—I'd be deemed unprofessional or insubordinate. Maybe that's what he wanted: to provoke an emotional outburst so I'd stop showing up.

Footnote: When the government launched Diversity, Equity, and Inclusion initiatives, it would have been helpful if they'd shared that with the people you would be working with—but that never happened. As a result, I spent much of my 35-year career working in spaces where I felt completely unwelcomed. Instead of being seen as a valuable team member, I was often treated like an inferior being—so they could feel superior. They didn't care that I had fairly bid on, and was awarded the contract. I was competent, and I earned it.

To any aspiring court reporter, I say this: keep showing up, no matter what they say or do—especially if you're Black. Just imagine what our ancestors endured during slavery all throughout the '40s and '50s. The confusion you see around you isn't in you—it's in them. Yes, you'll feel defamed. You'll feel wounded. The pain is immediate and sharp, like a fresh wound. But at some point, you may have no choice but to report those who try to tear you down just to feel better about themselves. Understand: people like that lack character and integrity. Otherwise, they wouldn't be acting the way they do. Some people are just innately evil.

That said, I want to be fair. Over the course of my career, I had the honor of working with more than 100 judges. Of those, only about eight had issues working with a Black court reporter—and they weren't shy about voicing it. That speaks volumes about the majority—those who respected The Rule of Law and honored their oaths.

Ironically, it was often the attorneys who felt superior and acted as though they were above the law—especially when it came to paying for services. Some felt that, because you were Black, your work should be free. Many Black attorneys paid late, became offended when held accountable, and paid only when they felt like it—sometimes four to five months later. It kept my business in collections mode. Eventually, I had to stop working with several of them because they simply weren't supportive.

My advice to aspiring court reporters is to focus on the positives—those little moments of progress and joy. Don't keep replaying the negative events that caused your business setbacks. That's tough, I know. When you dwell on what someone said or did, it brings the pain right back, and you relive it as though it happened yesterday. It can damage future working relationships.

What's wrong with reality TV is that even Dr. J. Phil can't help you with this—because first, he'd have to acknowledge that there's a real wall of racism that destroys lives. He'd have to admit that unless he's lived it, or won the fight against it, he can't truly help you. You'll be waiting a lifetime before someone like that admits the power games of racism in the workplace. No one wants to own it, yet it still wreaks havoc on the lives of Black professionals.

That's why you must learn to fight for yourself.

And if I leave you with nothing else: Document, document, document.

To own the fact that racism exists at all is the first step. You can't fix what you won't acknowledge. It's like going to the doctor and saying, "It hurts right here," while pointing to the source of pain—yet if the physician doesn't believe you, how can they treat what they refuse to accept? In that case, it's time to find another doctor. While psychology offers a generic fix to a deeply rooted problem, humanitarian efforts, sociological research and training, and a genuine respect for others should be mandated among diverse groups of people.

People are losing their homes, their cars, their families, their careers—yes, even their lives—because they've been caught in the traps of workplace harassment and violence. And we never truly address it until it's far too late. Ironically, we only begin to talk about it after a massacre occurs—labeling it another "isolated incident"—and we've had far too many of those in the last 20 or 30 years. We don't want to face the truth: that many of these individuals are deeply unwell—spiritually, mentally, emotionally—and if we had confronted the warning signs earlier, many of these tragedies could have been prevented.

Instead, we offer thoughts and prayers, hold candlelight vigils, and mourn the losses—while avoiding the harder work of getting help for those who commit the violence, even if they are judges, doctors, or attorneys.

We've seen renowned television psychiatrists who won't even touch the issue of workplace harassment, bullying, and intimidation—let alone the silent killers lurking in hostile work environments—for fear of losing ratings, viewers, or future invitations to analyze the next serial killer in the media circle. It's all about the Benjamins.

Case in point: the Virginia Tech and Arkansas massacres. In both cases, hatred festered like a pressure cooker waiting to implode. And when it finally did, we hid behind patriotic symbolism that turned into hollow displays of unity. We

105

hold hands, cry on camera, and perform a colossal show of "brotherly love"—only to return to business as usual once the media fades. The gestures are often more performative than they are sincere.

Racism of any kind, perpetrated by any group—Black, Asian or otherwise—against any people, is as cruel as death itself. As the Bible puts it, it is "as cruel as the grave." How do you justify such behavior? How can you claim to be a rational, prudent person while upholding systems of hate and oppression? Racism, at its core, is a **crisis of the soul**.

Amid all this confusion, not one renowned Black or White televangelist has spoken boldly on the topic of racism and workplace harassment. Why? For fear of being ostracized by evangelical colleagues or losing members of their congregation. And so, the silence continues. Nothing changes. Religious leaders stay quiet while oppression festers in the minds of would-be churchgoers, but that's not the true church—not the one God intended. That is the church of the god with the little "g."

I'm hard-pressed to believe that the saints—those who stand next to you in the choir stand every Sunday morning, dressed in fine linen and white robes symbolic of purity, singing songs to God—can transform into demons of destruction by Monday morning. Yet they wreak havoc in the workplace, behaving in ways that can only be described as hellish, while no man or woman of God dares to renounce it. That man's religion is in vain—Black or White, Hispanic, Jew, Greek or Gentile.

The condition of the soul—the inner man, the spiritual man—is what's truly at stake. The hidden Adamic nature just beneath the surface, has allowed politics and greed to seep into the church just as it has into the workplace, yet, we cannot fix what we refuse to own.

THE BATTLEGROUND

PART 3

Ispeak from experience and knowledge of the DEI initiative that is now being dismantled—not from what someone else told me. Moore Reporting Services has been awarded nearly 20 of these contracts in business and industry. I've participated in a number of women-owned, disadvantaged business contracts and know what it takes to bid on and successfully win one or more of these contracts. I remember when affirmative action was first implemented, and then came the phrase "Set Asides," followed by the inclusion of women and Black entrepreneurs—owners of small minority businesses—all driven by the Equal Employment Opportunity Commission.

It was an attempt to level the playing field for small business owners. Admittedly, there was much progress in the inclusion of many. However, during the early '60s and '70s, many didn't possess the skill sets needed to bid on local, state, or federal contracts; therefore, it was impossible for them to be included in the scope of work those contracts required.

After being awarded the contract, however, there was never enough help—typists or otherwise—willing to work for a Black woman-owned business. Many of my employees resented the knowledge I possessed when working with purchasing departments of the many local, state, federal, and governmental agencies. Being the first trailblazer in your community meant facing another wall you had to knock down. You had to constantly prove yourself—over, and over, and over again. It became a question of how many times you could afford to get knocked down and get back up before deciding to throw in the towel and move on.

It's a game of survival. Surviving the wall of racism, hatred, and bigotry that plays out in your life each day is no easy feat. I felt many times that writing the governor or senator was a necessary step. Holding them accountable for their Diversity, Equity, and Inclusion stats became part of the journey. I've worked with several governors who stood firmly behind diversity. Many believed the workplace should reflect the community—not just White people. Our communities are made up of many races, creeds, and ethnic groups. And in my town in Tennessee, we became the first state in the nation to dismantle DEI. That's an embarrassment for the great State of Tennessee. There are many other things I'd rather be first in, rather than being known as a source of hatred and division, while no other states have jumped onboard with this agenda.

Surviving the wall of dissolution, with a dream buried deep in your heart, forces you to step up to the plate and knock the ball out of the park. And if necessary, it's okay to write to the White House and share your plight in an attempt to hold detractors accountable. Many times, you'll find that behind the proverbial curtain of Oz is a jealous woman trying to sabotage your success as a contractor—even though you were the one invited to the DEI initiative, not them.

Women, we ought to be ashamed. We can do better. Attacking each other in the workplace, bullying, yes—even trying to kill, maim, or destroy one another—shows we haven't arrived yet. That's the conduct of a loser—one running in fear of herself.

Rather than respecting one another's visions and accomplishments, we tear each other down. It's the silent pain of low self-worth and low self-esteem that rears its ugly head when we see someone else succeed—and it isn't us. Honestly, I don't know how some of you sleep at night, or stand in the choir stand on Sunday morning after unleashing your jealous tirades throughout the week. This isn't the behavior of a winner—it's the mark of someone losing.

Until we own this, women will continue to be treated as second-class citizens while constantly losing ground. Life is not a game. The workplace is not a game. Professional relationships are not a game and should be off-limits. Someone has to say this, because we've allowed criminal behavior to penetrate the workplace so deeply that there is no longer a Rule of Law.

We're making it up as we go along. Many women are intoxicated with power and are abusing it in ways even most men wouldn't dare.

Biblically speaking, this has to be the spirit of Eve when she fell—wanting to be like God and usurping authority over Adam. That's not to say all women are evil, but we must take a hard look at our actions and the motives behind them. Satan himself became jealous of the worship God received in heaven and revolted—wanting power—and he was eventually cast out of heaven for abusing his power down to earth, and took on the form of a serpent.

Lastly, I'll say this: it is crucial that you become proactive rather than reactive. Use every option available to you. Know that no one is going to fight for you if you won't fight for yourself. People are just watching to see whether you'll lie down and take it or stand up and fight. I chose the latter. When I saw someone sabotaging my progress, I fought back. I addressed the issue—and the person who caused it.

However, this is a sensitive space. If not handled carefully, you can be labeled a troublemaker. It happens. The person who insulted you, or cursed you out, may turn around and get you fired—just because you confronted them – fight back. If necessary, report them to the GBI or the FBI. Get the investigation started.

At least during slavery, women shared the road to freedom with each other. Great women of the passage—Harriet Tubman, Mary Walker—pointed the way to liberty and democracy. Today, however, the path to equality is often blocked by fear and paranoia: fear that someone will take your place, fear that leads to sabotage among our own brothers and sisters.

Consequently, the most important battle you will fight is the one happening between your ears—your mind. What are you telling yourself? You must have the courage to file a grievance or formal complaint with the EEOC or your local Human Rights Commission. These agencies were created to help investigate age, race, and religious discrimination, unethical conduct, workplace violence, harassment, and terroristic threats—issues often left unaddressed.

Someone envisioned a day when you would need help pursuing a discrimination claim—and they fought to make the Civil Rights Act of 1964 a reality. Be grateful. Don't take that lightly. The very door that's now blocking your success is the same one others fought to open, so that you might have access to equal opportunity.

That's where we've gone so terribly wrong. No one's fighting legally anymore. People are fighting with guns, knives, and bombs instead of using the judicial system and the laws that exist. And that includes White-collar criminals, gang members, and anyone still stuck in trauma—from baby mama drama to absent father trauma—acting out in society, unable to function due to cycles of pain and underdevelopment.

I've seen it in court too many times. The perpetrator rattles off a list of excuses that all stem from their dysfunctional upbringing—an upbringing that, to them, seemed normal. Nowadays, the judicial system only comes into play after someone has taken matters into their own hands through vigilante justice—or after someone has been shot or murdered. That's when the judicial system steps in.

You have to learn how to pick your battles. With the blue wall of racism and injustice, you may find yourself fighting every day of your life, and often over the smallest, most mundane things—like the right to simply be yourself.

People will fight you just for being you in the 21st century, because they don't know who they are. And the truth is, many of them are carrying unresolved childhood issues into the workplace.

People who don't know who they are constantly measure their success by comparing it to others, because they are unhappy with themselves. Your success creates pain and confusion for them—especially if you're more successful than they are. They refuse to be happy for others. Happy people are generally happy for others. Unhappy people are generally unhappy for both themselves and others. Your joy reminds them of what they're missing—and what they're missing is the love of God.

You see it clearly in bad marriages. People go to great lengths to present themselves as happy, but underneath the

113

surface, they are miserable. I never was good at pretending, that's why I never went to Hollywood. Those with unhappy marriages often try to unravel someone else's marriage or disrupt the possibility of a new one forming. When they see two single people who could be a great match, they may even step in as a wedge—blocking the possibility of happiness for someone else—simply because they're unhappy at home with their own spouse or fiancée.

Their dissatisfaction spills over, and now they're sabotaging others' happiness because they're dissatisfied with their own lives. Often, they've compromised or settled for mediocrity. It's a spiritual condition, and it's dangerous. People unhappy in their own marriages often blame others for their discontent. They'll justify lusting after someone else's spouse—or a strong, successful single woman—by blaming her for their own indiscretions. "The devil made me do it." Yeah, right. Rather than take ownership for their behavior, the predator blames the prey.

Is it any wonder there are so many behavioral issues in the workplace? These unresolved issues creep into the office and taint professional relationships. It becomes all about control.

Predators are opportunists—often pretending to be happily married, but deep down, they are not. Single people, unite! It's time to drop the façade. You can be happily single. Jesus was single. Happy people want to see others happy. If you're happily married, it won't bother you to introduce someone to a good potential match. That's a sign of confidence and maturity, inner peace. But if you're unhappy in your marriage, you'll not only block others' opportunities, you'll also resent that someone you find desirable isn't available to you. These are often the cheaters, adulterers, and manipulators.

While it's natural to desire a healthy, fulfilling relationship, single people can sense when something is fake. That's why we're single—we're observing, analyzing, and testing unchartered territory while looking for the right mate. We're not rushing into a mistake we'll regret for the rest of our lives. It's like Tyler Perry's *Diary of a Mad Black Woman.* We don't want to become just another statistic—settling for a marriage of convenience that ends in divorce.

Single people need to stop coveting relationships that look good on the outside but are rotten underneath. Just because a relationship appears happy doesn't mean it is. Beneath the surface could be infidelity, emotional pain, abuse, or even disease. And yet, some people work hard to make you jealous of the lie they're living. I call them masters of manipulation.

Over the last twenty years, we've seen marriage unravel under public scrutiny, from governors to senators and local officials, infidelity has exposed the deception in high-profile marriages. Even reality shows like *Cheaters* pulled the curtain back on betrayal and confrontation. The rich and powerful will go to extreme lengths to cover up their affairs, fearing the loss of reputation and public image. But that fear—of losing their title as the "moral compass"—is a sickness in and of itself. They won't tell you they were at the freak-offs too.

They live with fear and guilt, terrified that the truth will come out. They don't want to admit that at 17 or 18, they made bad choices out of lust or immaturity. So, they bury the truth. They deny it. Because if the public really knew how badly they'd messed up, they'd lose their credibility and respect. So they pay people off to keep secrets. But we're all in the same boat. We've all done things we're not proud of. The details may be too painful or graphic to share, so we suppress them. And sometimes, the only reason we throw stones at others is to detract from our own brokenness.

Whether it's racism or relationships, we must begin looking inward—at the spirit of the man or woman we face in the mirror everyday.

This silent struggle to be honest with yourself is no easy task. At the end of the day, you're left with you. You must examine the intentions of those you allow in your life—and your own intentions as well—especially as you navigate the blue wall of racism and injustice.

If we would own our flaws, repent, and do the work to heal, we would all be better off. That would be a powerful starting point for addressing the secret sins we suppress everyday.

A SPIRITUAL AWAKENING

PART 1

You love your country, but through the eyes of the naysayer—and because of political division and bipartisan rhetoric—you'll never be patriotic enough. Your patronage and loyalty will always be called into question as long as the blue wall of hatred and hypocrisy exists.

Remember, you are not alone. Refuse to internalize the sickness that permeates the planet—God's planet. Refuse to wear the man-made labels people try to place on you. Though devastating, learn to love yourself enough not to internalize someone else's hatred of you. Leave them with their psychosis—don't carry it for them. Envision yourself as a survivor as you travel through life. Learn to enjoy life, as it is a gift that no man can fake or fabricate.

We are living in a world without balance, without identity, and without direction as we forge our way through this portal of time called life. No one tells you that life is a precious gift, not promised to anyone. And if you're blessed, you might live anywhere from 1 to 100 years on this earth—so make the best of them. Learn to bounce back. Learn to get up, brush yourself off, and keep going no matter the circumstances—even with the blue wall of hatred and disdain. Learn to look beyond the wall instead of staring at it continually.

Focus on the future.

Another element of Christendom that has failed humanity is the way religious leaders have minimized the wall. As a result, its limiting and diminishing effects on humanity have gone unaddressed—just under the radar. It now forms a kind of world religion of its own. We've cherry-picked what to address and what not to address in our religious dogma. This has caused society to spiral out of control, with false prophets twisting and manipulating the Word of God. We now have a generation of churchgoers who are spiritually lame and crippled, unable to stand, to make disciples, or to create, birth, and raise up entrepreneurs— while humanity hangs in the balance.

We shout. We run. We praise. But we return to work Monday morning staring at the same wall that divides us—and that no so-called man of God will speak on. Their colleagues and speaking engagements have become more important than the religious freedoms found in God's Word. I believe this is by design. False prophets know that if they empower the people, they themselves will be judged—and there would be nothing else left for them to do.

I've often wondered if it was deliberate—that the Word of God has been made of no effect. Powerless to set people free. Instead, the focus has been on building mega churches rather than creating true disciples. These churches have become spiritual holding pens—places of containment—failing to address the real crisis we face today.

We see this most clearly in the workplace, where the wall is most formidable—especially in harassment and discrimination. Yet with all the heated state and federal legislative debates, no one has challenged the so-called "right to work" laws. Even the pulpit on Sunday mornings shares nothing about why you don't have the right to life, liberty, and the pursuit of happiness on the workforce. You're on your own. What you receive is little more than rhetorical psychobabble that doesn't fit the crisis you're facing.

You often leave church unable to recall the sermon title—let alone how it applies to your circumstances. It may have been warm and fuzzy, highly sensational even—but it failed to address your reality. Workplace harassment is never discussed from the pulpit. Politics, however, is. And nowadays, pastors have so many issues themselves that they no longer have time for yours. Some say you're better off trusting your gut than seeking counsel from your pastor—especially when many have two or three families in the church, multiple girlfriends, and children born out of wedlock. Who would want that kind of destruction for their own family?

119

On the job, it often feels like a type of Egypt—a place of bondage and oppression. A place of mental torture at the hands of the same people you sang with in the choir stand on Sunday morning. However, by Monday morning, they've turned into demons from hell in the workplace— trying to get you fired for no reason other than jealousy. You struggle to maintain your emotional composure in the face of the abuse. And when you do address their absurd behavior, you're the one who gets blamed for what they did to you. The fact that you had the courage to defend yourself from their verbal onslaught becomes the reason they terminate you.

What I've learned from this is: it's God's way of using them to push you to your next level of success. He's guiding and ordering your steps. That's why it's important not to give up or give in—because God gets the last word. Know that it's the devil working through them, trying to make you abort the covenant you've made with God and the profession of your faith.

To that I say: stop running with the outer court Christians. Stop running with the Canaanites, the Hivites—you know, the wolves in sheep's clothing.

What you don't realize is that when you speak, they glare at you like you're from Mars—only because they see the God in you. This one was hard for me to understand, but in truth, they see the goodness of God, and it makes them uncomfortable. That's when the devil in them gets stirred up to wreak havoc in your life. Like Cain and Abel,

Satan comes to kill, steal, and destroy—your destiny, your finances, your joy, your peace. That's why you've become a target in the workplace. Learn to coexist with the devil's children. We used to call it platonic, keep it platonic. Know that you are the wheat, and they are the tares—grow together.

Yes, we live in 21st-century Egypt. That's a reality for some more than others. We're no longer being whipped and chained in brick pits, but the modern-day whip is isolation— being left out of mainstream society that doesn't want to acknowledge your existence. So we toil in silence, afraid to speak up against society's ills. It takes great courage to speak truth to power.

No matter how hard you try in the workplace, you may never be accepted by your peers—regardless of your Bachelor's or Master's degree. In the workplace, all is fair game. You'll do all the work, and they'll take all the credit. Expect to be harassed, undermined, and sabotaged—even as you put your best foot forward. Expect to see the promotion you earned handed to someone who slept their way to the top in the DA's office. Expect to see underachievers get ahead through nepotism. That's the kind of world in which we live.

There will always be someone who believes you don't belong, who thinks you shouldn't be taken seriously or even allowed to work. And often, you'll have more expertise than they do—which is exactly why you'll be singled out. They'll cast aspersions to appear more competent, even though they can't type 35 words a minute while you're typing 110 words per minute.

Be prepared for roadblocks and detours; and when you encounter them, get back up and get back in the fight.

One of the greatest life lessons from Egypt is this: you're going to have to learn to make bricks without straw—and still be expected to go the extra mile to stay employed. Expect little support, little appreciation, and almost no recognition. So you must learn to celebrate yourself. Encourage yourself. Pat yourself on the back. Don't wait for others to validate you. There's nothing arrogant about that. You have need of patience, be patient with yourself.

Your rejection is confirmation that you are like Jesus. "If they hated Me, they will hate you," Jesus said. "The servant is not greater than the Master."

Over the past thirty years, I've experienced some of the most formidable expressions of workplace harassment and discrimination imaginable—and in high places—all for no reason other than my race. And when it comes to women, your accomplishments don't matter. It doesn't matter that you struggled to get to where you are, just like they did. What matters to them is that you're perceived as a threat, your independence threatens them.

In truth, many don't want it on record what they're capable of. Many are liars, manipulators—even worse. That's why they don't want you in the workplace. They want to keep that hidden while casting aspersions on your character—with blatant lies they weaponize to justify why you're being removed or terminated. Only their accomplishments matter. Not yours. Is it too much to ask that we respect each other?

Being the first African-American court reporting business in my hometown—and the first to penetrate and desegregate the judicial system—is what qualifies me to write this manuscript. The fact that I've secured numerous DEI, Set-Aside, EEOC, and Affirmative Action contracts sets the stage for a story that must be told. If it weren't worth telling, someone would have already done it by now.

Desegregating the judicial system came with a great price—many trials, immense suffering, and several attempted murders, which are still under investigation as the cover-up continues. I've paid a price to be who I am, and I make no apologies. Workplace harassment and discrimination are indicators of a much deeper problem—one that can only be compared to the slave ships that bought and sold human beings along the Atlantic coast. There's been nothing in my life more comparable to slavery than what I've endured.

With each instance of hatred, I envisioned what must have happened to a slave tortured for no reason but the color of his skin—lynched for being Black. That's how I related my suffering to that of my ancestors. It kept me going and pressing toward my dream.

The overcoming spirit of the embattled slave became my point of reference. What I was going through had to be something similar.

I remember one occasion when the local bar association contracted my business to record the U.S. Senate debate, which was being held at one of our town's local convention centers. I was excited—thrilled, really—that my business had been selected to cover the debate. I wanted to look my best and do a good job, especially since every news outlet in the city would be there. So I closed my office early, rushed home, and went out to find the perfect business suit for the occasion.

Later that evening, I arrived at the hotel's assembly room to set up. First, I had to find my contact person with the bar association, who would escort me to the hall. Once we met, we walked to the doorway of the main hall and stepped inside. Just a few steps in, one of the event sponsors—representing a local newspaper—stormed up to us and shouted in a loud, insulting tone: "She's not staying in here! She's on your team! Take her with you!" He then forced us out of the room.

As soon as he realized I was a Black court reporter, he distanced himself, refusing us entry. The pain was immediate, intense, and agonizing. I did everything I could to keep my composure. I could tell that the bar association coordinator was deeply offended on my behalf—but she said and did absolutely nothing. Her face said it all: horror, shock, dismay. She was speechless.

This was just one of many examples of overt racial discrimination in the workplace that no one wants to admit still exists. This is why laws were put in place—to curtail the kind of blatant hate that continues to derail many small, minority, women-owned, and disadvantaged businesses.

As we stepped out into the lobby, it became clear that I would not be recording the debate that night—and for no other reason than the color of my skin. I knew what was coming next: she would tell me they didn't need me, and that I could go. But just as that seemed inevitable, one of the senator's attorneys approached and asked me to follow him to another area of the hotel—one where big-screen TVs had been set up—so I could record the debate from there.

When we arrived, however, the room was noisy and a bit rowdy, making it unsuitable for professional recording. So we eventually made our way back across the breezeway to the original assembly area.

This time, I was escorted into a small side room next to the main hall. Inside, were four White males watching the debate on several television monitors. The attorney opened the door and ushered me in. I began unpacking my equipment and was instructed to record the debate from a small, 19-inch television set crammed into the corner of the room where we all sat.

This was yet another moment of overt hatred that played itself out in a professional setting—where I was treated as a second-class citizen.

Once the lawyer left the room, the four men began asking questions: "Why did they call you?" "They didn't need you!" Adding insult to injury—but still, I sat quietly as the events unfolded. When the debate began, I recorded it, just as any true professional reporter would have.

Throughout the entire debate, the four men yelled at the television as though they were watching a sporting event, hurling insults at the opposing candidate. It made for a challenging assignment. When the debate was finally over, I packed up my equipment and left. I walked away with a new sense of spiritual awareness about racism and discrimination. It was a life lesson that left me emotionally anguished. Racism is as cruel as death itself, and I pray for the souls who practice it so loosely.

By the time I returned to the office, I could hardly speak. It was a somber, unforgettable moment—one I will carry with me for the rest of my life. I felt compelled to share it here in hopes that it might help someone else make it through their own difficult situations. The day had been an emotional roller coaster—highs and lows, peaks and valleys—leaving me completely drained and on the brink of depression.

I decided to phone my mom and tell her how things had gone at the hotel, only to break down in tears. The initial joy and elation, followed by the overt racism, the rejection, the taunting and rudeness—it had all taken a mental toll. The pure humiliation of it all—being passed around like a worthless pawn in a chess game. "They didn't want me there," I told my mother as I poured out my heart to her. By the time I finished, I felt completely exhausted and emotionally depleted by everything that had happened that evening.

This is when you have to call on your inner woman— the spiritual being within—remembering what the slaves must have endured as they cried out to God to intervene on their behalf.

A SPIRITUAL AWAKENING

PART 2

Nowadays, workplace restructuring is the mechanism institutions use when needing to reorganize, downsize, or RIF (reduce in force) employees. It's the term used for "right-sizing" a division or department. Today, we use the term *dismantling* as the term for the woke generation. No one can truly prepare you for the many terminations you will experience in life. No one ever tells you that you'll need at least two careers to survive the woke 21st-century workforce. In the '60s and '70s, it was honorable to work two jobs, but now it takes at least two careers as you matriculate through one dead-end job after another. You have to constantly remind yourself: the goal is survival.

You learn quickly that nothing is permanent. There was a time when you could retire from a job after 30 or 40 years with a great retirement check and a little money in the bank. Now there's age discrimination, and God forbid you become ill and have to file a worker's compensation claim—you're out the door. No questions asked. Today, everyone is dispensable. No one owes anyone anything, and longevity is a thing of the past.

We've survived the sub-prime lending crisis, hurricanes Gustav, Ike, Katrina, and Andrew, the Wall Street crisis, the foreclosure crisis, and now what's turning into an impending recession that may last five years or more. The economy teeters on collapse as we dismantle the federal government agencies that sustained us for half a century. State and local governments continue to implement budget cuts in healthcare and safety-net programs for the elderly and disadvantaged.

Criminals, driven by desperation, are angry and on the rampage—reacting to the idea of being hungry and homeless, living in tent cities indefinitely. Meanwhile, we sit in our homes, doors and windows secured with wrought iron bars, relying on high-tech alarm systems to shield us from crime just beyond our doorposts, as we try to figure out our next move in this maze of confusion and human demoralization.

Secondly, the church must take at least partial ownership of the dilemma in which this nation finds itself. The church has fallen asleep. Had it remained on its post—crying aloud and sparing not—rightly dividing the Word, we wouldn't see so much confusion. Today, everything once forbidden is now permissible, and what was once permissible is now forbidden.

Still, false prophets hunger for Learjets and mansions. Prestige and power have taken precedence over the welfare of God's people. With moral decay in their hearts, they frequent lascivious parties known as "Freak Offs," then return to the pulpit, sweating profusely, releasing ungodly spirits into the sanctuary—destroying the lives of the sheep.

No one talks about the rebellious spiritual leaders who don't realize their rebellion causes the sheep to rebel. It starts with the Head—Christ—and trickles down through pastors, bishops, and teachers. The body always takes on the spirit of its leader. So you'd better get to know Christ for yourself, or risk being led into a subpar life filled with rebellion. And we all know—rebellion is as the sin of witchcraft. Is your pastor engaged in witchcraft?

It's all about self-preservation now, as we witness the rise of Ponzi schemes in Christendom. We hear the latest gossip about pastors doing time in state prison for deceiving their congregations while riding around in Cadillac Escalades.

Even in church, pastors are competing with the sheep—jealous. And if iniquity rests in the pastor's heart, what are the people of God to do? Where is the 21st-century Moses? Where is the 21st-century Joshua? Is there truly a Word from the Lord—or are we being scammed at the altar?

To that, I say: you must have a personal relationship with Christ. Get to know Him for yourself—not for your pastor. Own your situation. Begin studying the Word of God so He can speak to you directly. God is no respecter of persons. Christ is the Head of the Church.

No one ever tells you why you were born into such a time as this—through God's portal called life, branching off through channels of time and light. Each season of life passes away and can only be measured in years, months, days, and hours—according to God's divine chronology. With every block of time comes the stressors of life. You watch yourself age: your steps shorten, your eyes dim, your hair turns gray, your teeth decay or fall out altogether. It makes you stop and consider what really matters in life. When you're young, you feel invincible.

But eventually, you begin to wonder: What's it all about? Why was I placed here in the first place? You realize you were chosen—and there's also an ETD, an *Estimated Time of Departure*. You learn to come to grips with that over time. So it behooves you to make the best of your allotted time. What should you be doing with your life? What is time for, anyway?

I've come to believe it's not how you came or went, but how you lived *in between time* that counts. You came from somewhere, and you're just passing through—on your way back to where you came from. Your spirit and soul will live on. Maybe your life is one big storybook—an episode in the cosmos, with each birthday marking a chapter in your life's story.

I'd even say the storybook of your life has a beginning, middle, and end—unfolding with each birthday. Each year turns a new page. What a beautiful analogy: that you're

131

living in time, a storybook that mirrors the *Lamb's Book of Life*. Where have I heard that before?

If your life is a type of *Lamb's Book of Life*, then your name was written in it long before you arrived. That means there's a final chapter awaiting—your ETA in eternity. You'll be held accountable for how you spent your time on earth. Time and eternity are synonymous. This has nothing to do with race or ethnicity.

At this point in my life, after all I've endured, I find it hard to believe that God sits in heaven choosing Black souls over White souls, or Hispanic over Asian. That's man's way—not God's.

If you were born, your name is in the *Lamb's Book of Life*—simply because you're living. God could have called it the *Book of Death*, but He didn't. It's life—what you're living now. Death is just the passage back to eternity. Just another portal.

The Creator and Cultivator of the soul has a larger, more magnificent plan for each soul harvested from planet Earth. When Adam became a living soul, so did we. *He that winneth souls is wise.* The power that governs the soul—which lives on eternally as we depart from a temporary life that cannot hold us on this side of eternity—belongs to God.

To go even deeper, the soul is the only thing that matters in the end—not the flesh. When you ponder the value of a soul, created by the Creator of the universe and placed on the earth in flesh formed from dust, you realize this flesh will return to that same dust, like it or not. Our bodies will one day be reduced to nothing more than a pile of earth.

There is, then, a kind of cultivating of souls—the precious fruit of the earth. And if you're not spiritually awakened, you'll make the mistake of only seeing people as fleshly images, idolizing the things of the world rather than the eternal. When you truly look at humanity, you don't just see faces or nationalities—you see souls, masses of them, passing through the birth canal of time on their way to a final resting place in eternity. It is a profound spiritual awakening.

So as we take in the temporary things of this world, we must not become overly burdened by a life that will eventually deliver us to a place called eternity—the final resting place of the soul. Could it be that a great harvesting and cultivating of souls is happening right under our noses? What a revelation! Those who live for the world—for things and material gain—can't comprehend this cultivation, because they're blinded by the temporary. It's not that they're any different from the rest of us, but they are entangled in the pursuit of wealth and status, which keeps them from seeing what's really happening around them. They lack vision and insight into spiritual things. Yet we are urged to desire spiritual gifts.

At one time or another, we've all lacked that vision. Some people don't know their purpose or destiny, all because their hearts are tied to the things of this world. This is where we must embrace one another and help open

133

the eyes of those lost in a sea of lasciviousness—with the Gospel of Jesus Christ.

Still, after all I've been through—the deferred dreams, reversed visions, the constant pursuit of knowledge, and the adversity of racism and the wickedness embedded in the world's systems—I came to the unequivocal conclusion that I had been chosen by God to be a trailblazer. I was called to help ease the pain of racism and despair in the workplace through the penning of this book.

Is it any wonder that only by acknowledging, owning, and overcoming life's hardships can we experience the true triumphs that are intricately connected to our most difficult moments? We owe it to the next generation to run this race with endurance, so we can pass on a meaningful and life-changing legacy. Because even when you put your best foot forward, racism will show up—especially if you're a dreamer.

A SPIRITUAL AWAKENING

PART 3

One moment of youthful indiscretion can lead to a lifetime of pain and hardship—and in many instances, you may never recover. This is what they don't tell you. You wake from a one-night stand to find out that you are now HIV positive or pregnant, both of which carry enormous lifelong consequences. And God forbid the man you slept with was married—or that you've contracted genital herpes or another incurable disease from one night of pleasure. Satan goes about the business of entrapping the saints into believing that sin doesn't have consequences.

It's unfortunate that we often must travel the road of crisis in order to change our way of thinking. Men need annual health screenings for STDs just like women do. In many cases, it is the man who is carrying the disease from woman to woman. We now see women being infected at alarming rates, as some men choose to be intimate with both men and women. There seems to be no correction for the out-of-control alpha male—but don't let him entrap you for life.

While watching television one night, I was struck by a world-renowned pastor who, while in the pulpit, began a discussion about women and abortion. Like many women of God, I respect anyone who calls themselves a man or woman of God, so I was eager to hear what he had to say. He had always seemed to handle women's issues fairly and with a degree of impartiality, reminding us that women also have work to do for the Kingdom. But I'm always amazed when I hear men speak on women's issues as though they were women themselves. It's almost laughable—from pregnancy to abortion—the narrative is often depicted as a one-sided love affair, quite like the story of the woman caught in adultery. I call it tunnel vision. Her accusers were all men. Her lovers were all men. Yet the responsibility for her conduct was placed squarely on her shoulders, not theirs.

We often see a generic approach to men's behavior, while their actions are dismissed with phrases like, "a man will be a man." There is absolutely no accountability.

As the pastor began his charismatic rant—"Drop it like it's hot, drop it like it's hot"—I thought to myself, *drop what like it's hot?* The phrase was a cliffhanger, so I sat on the couch, waiting for clarification. It turned out he was speaking about women and abortion. My mind immediately flashed to the story of the woman caught in the very act of adultery. I imagined Jesus addressing the abortion debate just as He did then: "He who is without sin, let him cast the first stone." Women don't impregnate themselves—men do. And as such, they must be held accountable too.

Just as that woman was left to be stoned to death while the man was seemingly exonerated, many pastors across this nation stone women from the pulpit every Sunday for issues that are, in truth, men's issues—control issues—conveniently reframed as women's issues through misrepresentation. In the 21st century, we see so-called pastors with ten or more children by various women in their churches, yet nothing is ever imputed to the man's conduct.

One day we're "loosed," and the next day, we're "not so suchy-much." Personally, I never bought into any of it. To me, it was a big hoax. Eventually, the truth always rises to the top. The message was riddled with spiritual schizophrenia: "I want you to go," but then "don't go just yet." "Find your identity in Christ," but also "sit there and wait until I say move." This conflicting approach keeps women bound rather than truly loosed to the freedom God's Word provides—freedom that leads to self-sufficiency and abundant living.

I was so moved by the pastor's ridiculous rant that I decided to write another well-known pastor to express my disdain for the one-sided interpretation of scripture— blaming the woman entirely for the story of adultery. Before a woman could ever "drop it like it's hot," some man had to drop it like it's hot first. Terms and phrases like that are not in the Bible. False doctrine. False narrative. That's why

I eventually stopped supporting that ministry—it wasn't grounded in scripture.

And yet, the dominant male—sperm donor and all— never bears the brunt of these dogmatic attacks that target women every Sunday. Women squirm in their seats under sermons designed to impugn them while the man walks free, rarely held accountable for the life he helped create. Jesus called this *righteous indignation,* and He once asked, "Why trouble ye this woman?"

The woman is often depicted as some self-consumed feminist who chooses to abort her child with no conscience, when in reality, the decision is far more complex and painful. After forty years of working within the judicial system, I've seen young college students frequently petition the courts for legal terminations under hardship petitions.

And yet, we exploit the woman's right to seek legal recourse while never hauling in the man to sit beside her in court—though he participated equally in the act. The woman is left holding the bag while the man moves on to his next conquest, continuing this cycle of irresponsible, unchecked behavior. We must teach our young men how to possess their bodies with honor and obedience to God's Word, not in riotous rebellion. Their bodies are temples of the Holy Ghost—and that alone should give them pause before stepping into fatherhood.

We've failed to stress the sanctity of marriage and the divine calling of fatherhood. These gaps contribute directly to the breakdown of the family.

Again, women don't impregnate themselves. Men need to get real and come clean with God and the church, and stop using the scriptures to tip the scale in favor of men. God is no respecter of persons. The dominant male is out of control. In many instances, the church has taken on the persona of a nightclub—a place to hook up and look for a partner.

A perfect example of supporting immorality is the way some have twisted the relationship between David and Jonathan, stretching scripture out of context to imply they were lovers. There is absolutely no record or inference that God condones or supports homosexuality. A more accurate term for such misinterpretation is *paganism*.

I've heard this preached by immature pastors—many trapped in the closet themselves—trying to seduce others into believing that sodomy is accepted by God. But we know what God did to Sodom and Gomorrah. To interpret scripture as though it were subject to private interpretation is an abomination. Scripture is of no private interpretation. It speaks clearly on matters of morality and immorality.

With so many political figures caught surfing the Internet for child pornography, soliciting sex from underage boys, trafficking children, and attending freak-offs, is it any wonder that the "alternate lifestyle" has gained such momentum in this nation? In a court of law, this is called solicitation of sodomy.

I'm certain that if God took the time to tell us directly that Judas was a devil, He would not hesitate to declare His detest for the conduct of Sodomites. There are no references in scripture to the Apostle Paul—or any other Apostle—being immoral. Instead, they moved under the power of the Holy Spirit and preached against such behaviors. The scriptures are not silent on this topic. Don't hate the messenger.

The purest form of *philos* love—like that between David and Jonathan—has been perverted by those who lack sound hermeneutical understanding. When someone who has not been taught the Word properly assumes the role of a teacher, the result is vain imagination, not divine revelation. There's a big difference between vain imagination and being led by the Holy Spirit. And no, the phrase "the disciple whom Jesus loved" does not mean that John was a homosexual—it simply denotes a close spiritual bond.

Can you imagine the confusion if we were to greet the brethren with a holy kiss in this day and age? Taken out of context, even that would be misunderstood.

Unequivocally, men have a hard time correcting other men. They are more concerned with their role of headship than with obeying God's Word and leading by example. Is it any wonder that so many of our young Black males walk around with their pants hanging down, exposing their boxer shorts? To that I say: total rebellion.

Worse yet, many are incarcerated. Still, no man wants to step up to correct these out-of-control, immature dominant males. Until we properly teach and apply scripture, the church will never become the *true* bride—not the bridegroom—that our Creator intended. Only the Word of God can change these young men. But with the woke generation and unrepentant pastors and bishops attending freak-offs instead of leading by example, we continue to suffer loss: loss of family, loss of life, loss of intimacy with God. We've made the Word of God of no effect. We blaspheme God's Word.

We bring shame to God's Word when we refuse to be doers of the Word and not hearers only.

At its core, immorality is a loss of identity and a national crisis. Men are losing direction. Women are losing direction. All of us have the capacity to fall back into our old Adamic nature, like the Israelites did at the foot of Mount Sinai. But if you're truly born again, you do not allow the Adamic nature to override what you know to be God's will for your life. Anyone can fall—but the redeemed rise again.

Where we often go wrong is that we meet people while they are still running from God, like Jonah. We capture a mental snapshot of them in that season, then hold it encrypted in our hearts for years. By the time they find salvation 20, 30, even 40 years later, we pull out that old image and use it against them—despite God's redemption. Our foolish hearts condemn them. We push them away from God.

To those who are guilty of false confessions and railing accusations, know that you will be held accountable. Satan is the accuser of the brethren—and the sisters too. Stop

141

letting Satan use you to destroy the faith journeys of others. You are not God. You do not know these people.

Meanwhile, from pulpits across the country, we hear fables and stories—"Why did the chicken cross the road?"—useless, meaningless distractions that benefit no one but the speaker. People are dying on the pews right next to us—struggling to pay their bills, keep their homes, keep their cars. And we sit more desperate than ever for a true Word from the Lord. It's one of the greatest mockeries ever perpetrated on the people of God.

The anointed cherubs who once delivered powerful Words now preach stale sermons. There's no fresh oil. Nothing pure. Nothing new. We're fed the same old soup—warmed over and over—and we wonder why people fall into apostasy, counted as sheep for the slaughter. We've become more fascinated with the *personality* of the pastor than with the *person* of God. And often, the one who has suffered the most carries the deepest anointing.

As the pastor continued to humiliate women from the pulpit, I grew increasingly incensed at the thought of a man trying to dictate what a woman should or shouldn't do with her body—in an open forum, no less. What about adolescent girls who have been raped by their fathers, brothers, child molesters, or family acquaintances? Now they must choose between life and death—carrying the seed of their attacker, fearing the unknown, likely raising the child alone.

This is a diversion—a tactic men use to take the heat off themselves, particularly those hiding secret sins like molestation or inappropriate touching. So we focus on condemning women for abortion rather than addressing child rape and holding perpetrators accountable.

Because, after all, the pastor won't be there when the music stops, the curtain closes, and the crowd goes home. The young girl will be left to relive her trauma for the rest of her life. Yet we hear no broad, empathetic message that covers this reality.

And what if she's carrying the child of her stepfather, biological father, uncle—or yes—even her pastor? As that pastor ranted, I sat in disbelief. How insensitive can one be?

I've heard it said before: *Now that'll preach!* But I thought, no—it won't. That pastor won't be there to help raise the child. He won't be paying child support. To him, it was just "a good Word." He never stopped to consider the woman's emotional, physical, or psychological pain. So I just sat there… listening.

I'm of the opinion that women don't take abortion lightly—at least not as lightly as this pastor would have you believe. All you have to do is watch the faces of the audience in the room. The room will often fall silent when the truth is being stretched or distorted—especially the truth of the scripture—and there is little to no appreciation for one-sided sermons. A 'holy hush' often falls over the apathetic women, a silence that comes from the very heart of God, as the shouting ceases and no one says, "Amen."

A SPIRITUAL AWAKENING

PART 4

Yet another day, while sitting in my office listening to a local radio broadcast about the federal funding of abortion, I decided to write the White House about this topic. Funding, in itself, is nothing more than a way to promote the cause of the out-of-control dominant male that no one seems to have the courage to confront. Rather than holding him accountable for what he does with his body—which ultimately costs the government money—they give him a free pass.

Lately, they have begun confiscating driver's licenses, but these men still need to drive in order to work, to pay child support and alimony. So with the pastor's depiction of women "dropping it like it's hot," what's a true woman of God to say? I chose to write and give input into what remedies could be helpful when it comes to funding abortion.

To fund abortion or not to fund abortion—that is the question. It's a hot-button issue in our nation today. On a national level, abortion and federal dollars are like mixing oil and water. The bigger question is: what do we do with the body of a woman who has now become pregnant by a sperm donor? Do we spend federal dollars on abortion? Rather than tell the dominant male, "If you play, you have to pay," we've allowed him to sidestep responsibility. None of us have the right to procreate without taking responsibility for our actions, and then simply walk away. We should legislate law in this matter. Better yet, let's just make it a woman's issue, while impugning the male.

Our government is already overburdened with welfare and food stamp recipients, and other federal programs. At least such legislation would force people to think before they act—an exercise in self-restraint, which should be taught at home during puberty. No one should be allowed to wreak havoc in our communities, leaving fatherless babies all over the globe with absolutely no accountability. And the best-kept secret is that many of our nation's children are being fathered by religious leaders as well. So we're forced to "play church" and show our approval for what the Bible calls an infidel—a man who doesn't take care of his own home—but we don't want to hurt anybody's feelings.

At first conception, the parties should take a DNA test to determine paternity, and it should be law. From that moment on, you're either going to step up and take responsibility for the poor choices you've made—pro-choice or not—

or you're going to be fined and/or imprisoned until you decide. Especially if the government is expected to assist with raising your children, then you should be required to reimburse them for medical care and child support at some point in the future. Now that's taking responsibility. This should be made known at the outset.

It's such an awesome responsibility—and a maturing one as well—to see someone standing before a judge faced with the prospect of accepting fatherhood or motherhood because of their own behavior. I've witnessed these proceedings in court numerous times. It's not until then that the proverbial light bulb goes off: "Look at the mess I've gotten myself into." And truthfully, who wants to be dragged into court and forced to stand before a judge, and ultimately forced to pay child support—let alone go to jail? It's a no-brainer.

I'd venture to say this would stop a lot of playing without paying, especially if it became public record that you have a history—if you topped the list for fathering multiple children via the state's Vital Statistics Archives and Vital Records Division—and then left them to fend for themselves without paying or parenting. Even if it's a woman, she too should be held accountable for her irresponsibility. Correction is needed at all levels.

We have a local paper in our town called *Busted*, which shows the faces of people who have been convicted of petty crimes, misdemeanors, thefts—and they've been posted in this paper in an attempt to shame them into consciousness and help change their behavior. And not only them—there ought to be a public registry or newspaper that exposes the out-of-control male who is procreating beyond three children within a community, to give women notice about what this guy's really about.

It's criminal what's being done to women and children. She's forced to raise children alone because she's been preyed upon by some womanizer thinking only of himself, his own interests, his own desires—leaving the destiny of the woman in shambles. Now that will preach! So why isn't it being done? And with no preacher expounding on this dilemma on Sunday mornings, they instead turn the Bible into Aesop's Fables and fairy tales. And what's ironic—it never registers until there are children involved. Then everyone wants to repent and turn to Jesus—but for how long? People should be taught to consider their consequences, starting with the preacher.

The church should preach, "Stay in your lane." But they can't—because they know they themselves are guilty of straddling the fence, and so are the deacons—all things male. I can't forget the day I went down to join the church one Sunday, and just as I reached the altar, I heard one of the deacons say, "This one's mine. You got the last one." That's when I thought to myself, *What have I done?* I should've observed a little longer before making the trip down to the altar. Too late now.

From that point on, I became a new member observer. And as luck would have it, at a church meeting that was called, the preacher was being asked to step down for inappropriate conduct on a church outing in Florida—at the pool. It was too late to put it in reverse, so I hung around for a year or two. It was nothing like I'd imagined it would be—or should I say, should have been. He turned out to be a super stud. Eventually, several women at the church who were sleeping with him got into what I'd consider a church fight—his first wife and his mistress—as I eased on out the back door. The church eventually fell off and now hardly has any members. It's like a ghost town.

So Sunday morning church has become one of the most significant places to be—but yet, the least influential. We're powerless to make the necessary changes in our lives because leadership is powerless to lead—let alone set any examples of what church and family are supposed to resemble. Who wants to go to church and be disrespected by women laying around with preachers and deacons, and laypeople who've allowed the church to become sexualized in order to control the masses? I know I don't—and if that's the prerequisite for membership, I'm done.

We're powerless to deal with the ills of our day. And since we've had no support mechanisms ourselves when coming up as children, we're refusing to support others. It's not that we can't support others—we just choose not to, especially if they're doing better than us. We're consumed with wrong ideas, wrong thinking patterns, and even confusion about what love is—because the pastor wasn't taught. Now, he can put on a show, he can perform for you—but he never went to seminary or allowed himself to be taught about *agape*, *eros*, and *philos* love. So we're all limited. And for how long will you allow someone who's ignorant beyond a 10th-grade level of education to preach to you? We are instructed to grow in grace and in knowledge.

Most of the love we've been exposed to can be considered worldly love—*eros* love, sensual, sex-driven love. So when we see expressions of real love, like *storge* love (what's known as family love), it's hard to relate. Especially for those of us raised in single-parent households, we're often slow to catch on to how this thing called love is supposed to go. After all, we've never seen any roles played out with the "happily ever after" endings that so many authors use to close their fairy tales.

So we think, *If it's not someone in my family or a close friend, I don't care how gifted you are—you're not doing it here.* "My wife is jealous"—his second wife, the one who beat the tar out of his first wife so she could be called 'First Lady.' I'd submit, you'd better learn how to trust God for yourself. Get in His Word and establish a personal relationship with God, and stop leaning on ungodly people for guidance and direction—people who don't want to see you soar to the next level in your life, but would rather block your pathway to destiny.

Church choirs used to be phenomenal and spirit-filled when God was first, but now, "Ichabod" is on the doorpost—for the glory of God has left the temple, and

God is not welcomed in many churches. I truly believe this is why there's a great falling away.

Even pastors and deacons with unresolved childhood issues often reveal it in the way they love their congregations. You can see where they fall short in the love department by how they encourage some and discourage others. They support some but not others. They abuse some but not others—in open forum. Personally, I consider it a sickness that exists in the church, not in the workplace. It is a spiritual awakening.

All you have to do is listen to the sermon, and you will hear over and over again: "my mom, my mom, my mom." Never, "my dad and I," or "my dad this," or "my dad that." If you listen closely with your spiritual ear, you can hear the love-starved child crying out from the soul—impoverished, longing for male bonding and companionship that only a father could give. Still, they move on to repeat the cycle of abuse and rejection, lacking the male bonding needed to lead and live successful lives—and are angry because God blessed *you.*

Some will go so far as to blaspheme the power that's on your life rather than offer support for God calling you into the ministry. They believe that if they reject you long enough, you'll abort your ministry and fall away into apostasy. Dejection—that's the plan they have for you. All because they can't dictate who God should or shouldn't call, and they're mad at God because He called *you* at all— while denying the power that's on your life.

People will set themselves against you like Ahab and Jezebel, calling and honoring who *they* would call rather than who *God* has called. The true saints of God are a work in progress. Learn to embrace the good, the bad, and the ugly. Embrace the work God is allowing to come your way. God already knows how it's going to turn out. It's your job to believe that as long as you're in God's will, everything is going to turn out all right. Just don't let the enemy razz you—your blessing is just on the other side of this trouble. Make up your mind that you will not faint until you see the glory of God turn things around in your favor. Keep pressing.

I've seen several pastors go to great lengths to cause you to doubt your calling. They go about the business of poisoning the minds of their ministerial staff and parishioners against the power that is on your life—and they claim to be on their way to heaven. Many times, it's because of envy and jealousy.

I've done this once or twice in my life—when I was a teenager. I didn't know how to say *no,* so I hung around people who were horrible influences. Looking back now, I know it had to be God who kept me from Satan's traps that had been set to ensnare me—before I came to myself, before I had the courage to stand up and live for Christ. Inwardly, I wasn't ashamed of God—I just feared being ostracized and rejected by my peers. I did some crazy stuff on my way to finding my purpose. If anyone hates you for no reason, it's because they are not saved themselves. They will set traps, scheme, and backbite to influence the minds of people who don't even know you. They want your good name. They're after your reputation. This is why they gossip about things they don't know, because they see your progress—and they see that you have the favor of God on your life.

It wasn't until I finally said *no* to my bad influences—my haters—and walked away from those toxic relationships that my life began to turn around for the better. I'm forever grateful to God for allowing me to come to myself before it was too late. Now that I'm saved, I've never been more hated. I had to turn away from unsaved family members, loved ones, and friends who were in full-blown rebellion against God. I was given the opportunity to get back on track in my early 20s. And anybody who brings up something you did at 17 or 18 is not your friend. They're holding you hostage to your past in order to circumvent your future.

I've watched their children murder people. I've seen their family members fired for stealing—on the 6:00 news. But they won't tell you that about *their* lives. They're willing to cast aspersions on others while suppressing the failures in their own families.

I'm convinced that the 21st-century church has gone a-whoring from the mandates of God—contaminating and being contaminated. That's why it's not wise to judge a person before they come to themselves. They were lost then, searching for their purpose, casting their pearls before swine—which took them farther than they wanted to go. Some never make it back, let alone come to themselves.

And when you reflect back on the pagan society in the Old Testament, you'll find they committed adultery, murdered, and aborted—or sacrificed—their children on the different altars of their day. They even ate them for food. They participated in orgies, sexual immorality, and other perversions. They worshipped idols of silver and gold. They knew nothing of God's love or His righteousness and were consumed with the lusts of this world, worshipping false gods.

One thing you've got to learn: Jesus was delivered up because of envy, so the servant is not greater than the Master. You will be hated by man. Just consider the suffering as confirmation—an honor and indeed a privilege—to be counted among the righteous who are traveling along the narrow road that leads to the Kingdom, rather than the broad road that leads to destruction and hell.

It's not the pastor's job to control the saints—it's the Word of God's job to do that. The behavior of the people illustrates just how much Word a person does or does not have operating in their life.

Churchgoers who are facing challenges with stealing and lying might need to check out the spirits that are speaking into their lives. I believe this is where we've gotten off track—wrong spirits speaking into our hearts. Say you know that stealing is wrong and there's absolutely no way you would be found guilty of such an act, and then you find yourself at the grocery store and suddenly feel the urge to steal. You don't know where it's coming from—perhaps it's a mere compulsion—yet it's there. You wrestle with the thought and quickly cast it out of your mind. If this has ever happened to you, there's a good chance that someone who is speaking into your life transferred that spirit to you. If you're struggling with lust and know it's a problem, you might need to examine the person who is influencing your life. If you are overcome with hate, envy, or jealousy, it's worth checking the company you're keeping. That's how important it is to God. Beelzebub cannot cast out Beelzebub. Learn to listen intently to what your spirit is saying, and you will find that in many instances, someone with major sin issues is dropping seeds of discord and discontent into your spirit—sending your life off course.

This is where I say: be not dismayed. Your reward is not going to come from them anyway—it will come from God. Continue to wait on God as He works His plans for your life. You'll begin to see that you can endure tough times just by knowing God's Word. It's better to know what God is doing in your life than to not know. When we don't know the plan of God for our lives, we make irrevocable decisions that can permanently change the path set before us. I know—I did.

When I rebelled against what was right and chose to hang out with people who didn't mean me any good, things got really bad. And with all of that, I was still unhappy— basking in sin, pleasure for a season—all to be with the crowd.

The good part is, I can count the number of times over the years when I was living dangerously close to the edge with the crowd, yet God never allowed me to fall. Instead, He came and delivered me from those people—in the nick of time—only for me to find that they were lost and without purpose. Once I walked away from those negative influences and was no longer a follower, I realized how badly they had needed me. They needed me more than I needed them. What I didn't understand then was—they were miserable.

It takes courage to walk away. Know that your pain has a purpose, designed by God to build a mighty testimony in your life—just like the plight of Joseph, which was to keep many people alive.

Know there is a greater plan orchestrated by God that you are fully able to endure. With each trial, as your purpose unfolds and the storms quiet down, you'll see that you have made it through. Now you have demonstrable power in your testimony—power to encourage others that they can make it too. If God allows it, He will see you through it. Learn to see yourself on the other side of trouble—on the other side with victory. That's the way He guides us. Where He leads, you can rest assured that He will shield, protect, and defend you.

To become the target of the wicked is confirmation that you are a true child of God—or they wouldn't be meditating on you. A true child of God has no desire to target anyone, especially not the wicked. You'll never see it happen the

155

other way around. Know that when you are targeted, it's a sign that the person targeting you is likely unhealthy mentally and deeply unhappy. Happy people don't target people. Healthy, mentally sound people don't do it either. Only cowards, bullies, and discontent individuals behave that way.

Know that victory is just on the other side of your experience—and this too shall pass.

The condition of the wicked heart is only evil continually—total depravity. They operate from a distorted emotional state that sees you as a threat to their livelihood. They function in paranoia. Translation: they are miserable. And the proof of their misery is their obsession with you. So I say—keep your focus on God and let God take care of the wicked. Targeting others only reveals a lack of understanding of God's Word. And if you were to ask them why they're targeting you, they wouldn't be able to explain it.

Because envy is as cruel as the grave, expect your enemy to be just as cruel. Know that envy is rottenness to the bones. Your enemy's bones are rotten to the bone marrow.

Instead, let your light continue to shine brightly. As theirs dims and becomes obscure, you'll see it in their eyes. The pain shows up there—it's a look of confusion and dismay. But in your case, so much light shines from your countenance that it distracts them. Your praise is electrifying, and they try to interfere with what God has called you to do—to distract you from becoming who God intended you to be.

Make no bones about it—the person sabotaging your destiny in the workplace, in your career, and even in the church—is working for the devil.

Just like Pharaoh, a brother is born for the day of adversity. God will harden whomever He chooses in order to get the glory out of your situation. We must be patient and let God have His perfect will in us.

In my field, I've witnessed thousands of instances from the witness stand where people have allowed the enemy to rise up in them, sabotaging others in the workplace for no reason but jealousy. I've even had to fight those battles myself—numerous times—when coworkers were on assignment from the devil to disrupt the plans God had established for my life.

Over the past forty years, I've found this to be true: the world is filled with power-hungry people at all levels of society—people to whom power has been vested, yet they have no idea what to do with it. That is made evident by the way they abuse it when dealing with others in the workplace. They use their power for evil, not good. They're so intoxicated by their positions that they will design negative situations, entrap, seduce, and harass subordinates—all to create hostile work environments and vilify you.

I've seen it so often that they're easy to detect—it's clinical. It's generational. It has a repetitive momentum from generation to generation, but it's the same force propelling their behavior: evil. What has happened is they have brought their childhood issues, formative years, and dysfunctional upbringing into the workplace—much of which caused them to feel helpless—and now they have power that they're using to derail other people's destinies.

Power in the hands of a fool is a dangerous thing. People who were taught to hate at an early age are now sitting in judgment of your dreams and accomplishments.

It's hard for them to distinguish between the fact that they don't actually *own* the company or the business—they just work there, like you do. And like them, you have a home and family to provide for as well. That's why I never understood the concept of workplace harassment and discrimination. The practice is for losers. What kind of pleasure are you deriving from that behavior? The perpetrators of this behavior are nothing more than employees themselves, yet somehow feel emboldened to act out in the workplace as though it were an obligation—a duty of some sort.

We keep dismissing it as some kind of privileged behavior, depending on who you are in the workforce. Their refusal to work as a team—working *with* someone rather than *against* them—indicates they have a competitive spirit. The root cause often stems from what they were taught about how to relate to others. Everyone entering the workplace should have a sense of servitude and mutual respect—first for the company, then for their coworkers—as they work together as a team for the benefit of the organization.

That's why you have to be prepared to study the types of minds you will ultimately encounter in the workforce. Just like in church, not everyone is there for the right reason. The truth is, Satan goes to church—but he also goes to work. Maybe it's human nature that's consumed us—preoccupied us with our neighbors rather than the tasks at hand. This kind of negative conduct plays a significant role in determining who becomes an employee and who becomes an entrepreneur in life.

Know that it's a spiritual dilemma. When you take pleasure in the destruction of others—it's spiritual. Somewhere in their youth, they lacked structure and support from godly role models, and they now truly believe that their conduct in the workplace is acceptable. When in reality, it's not. It's totally unacceptable.

THE COURAGE TO PERSEVERE

While we're glad that our children are partaking of the fruits of the labor of the Civil Rights Era—largely due to those pioneers who paved the way to where they find themselves—I'm afraid they don't even understand the struggle: the marches, the protests, the sacrifices that opened the doors to where they are today. And so, we now see the disrespect and rude conduct—toward self and others—being played out in society by the children of the movement.

The disgrace that haunts all of us is when we see Black mayors, Black pastors, Black representatives engaging in embezzlement and scams—acts that are not only sacrilegious and profane but also abominable blasphemies against God. We overcame, yes—but not to become common criminals and thugs, rank sinners before the God who delivered us out of the hand of Egypt. Is this how we thank God for removing our shackles and chains? God forbid!

Somehow, we've managed to dismantle the bridge that carried us across to the next generation, and to do that is to

160

disrespect the slaves who forged freedom's pathway. On the backs of slaves, we have been literally carried into the 21st century. Yet our children's unfamiliarity—or inability to relate—to the struggle has them fighting one another, behaving like a people devoid of purpose, destiny, and calling. History has its place.

Is it merely a lofty notion to envision a people who have passed the torch of enlightenment to the third and fourth generations in order to improve their way of life and survival techniques? One could only imagine a world where everyone is connected to their identity, vision, and purpose. What a grandiose idea. It is only when the youth of our day suffer great loss that they embrace history—and depending on the condition of their hearts, they may very well find themselves acting like the oppressor.

Nowadays, we find few traveling the narrow road, and fewer still surviving long enough to get through it and tell their stories to the world. And for those narrow road travelers, we bid you Godspeed. If the wall of racism doesn't take you out, your Canaanite brothers and sisters just might—so look for it. Sibling rivalry continues to rear its ugly head, from Cain and Abel until now. It's true: when you can't celebrate someone else's successes and victories, it's a good sign you're immature, and not ready yet. It's only when you can be happy for someone other than yourself that you begin to discover who you really are.

This new generation's eyes are eschewed by their own rebellion. They're deeply connected to rap, hard rock, and

161

even Satanic music lyrics that lead them down a path of destruction. The illicit sex videos—dancing and prancing about—resemble soft porn, all traps of the enemy. And for some, they may never recover and don't even know it yet. The face of the enemy is someone preying on the way they think at an early age, before they understand the gravity of what's right and wrong in the music industry—all to make money at the expense of our sons and daughters. It's a racket. And if bought into before maturity, you can be lost for an entire lifetime.

DICHOTOMY OF PSYCHOLOGY

———⊃•✸•⊂———

Learning to embrace racism and discrimination is a strategy—a strategic concept that has never been taught by any psychiatrist—and can only be taught by someone who has experienced the aftermath and onslaught of the pain of racism and discrimination in the workplace. It requires a hands-on approach, which is why we see so few psychiatrists who possess the skill set or the willingness to take ownership and tackle the single most powerful and pervasive issue in our society today. Instead, they choose escapism, saying, "I have Black friends," seemingly hoping that precludes them from being called a racist.

I'd say, learn how to make racism work for you instead of against you—that's what I call the Dichotomy of Psychology. It's a concept that cannot be embraced or taught by psychologists because, first, you can't teach what you don't own. You can't heal if there is little ownership of the sickness or disease. Many psychologists often treat the victim, not the perpetrator. And because they themselves have never been victims of racism and discrimination, they

163

choose denial—escapism—about the reality of it and the harm it causes in the workplace, stereotyping others rather than providing solutions. It's impossible to teach what you yourself are guilty of.

Escapism is when you have been assaulted in the workplace, and rather than confronting the perpetrator, you confront the victim—as though they did something wrong. That is the coward's approach. Too much of this is happening in our society today. We beat up the victim because we don't have the courage to confront the perpetrator.

They'd have to own it first in order to help you heal emotionally, psychologically, and otherwise. Could you imagine someone attempting to dismantle the layers and layers of pain and suffering that have been inflicted over time—but who can't own the fact that they themselves practice racism and discrimination? What a hoax.

I've seen it hundreds of times from the witness stand: in family therapy, rape crisis centers, crime victim therapy, and child molestation cases—the list goes on. But when it comes to the effects of racism and discrimination on individuals, there is absolutely no counseling. That's quite convenient. To say nothing at all is to silently acquiesce. Behavioral issues—like those invoices being tossed into the trash can by the sick administrator—are ignored. To that, I say: we should never allow ourselves to turn a blind eye and deceive ourselves into believing the lie that racism and discrimination are okay, or that we should just learn to live with them. Unfortunately, that's what you often must learn to do—make adjustments just to get along. But whenever and wherever possible, own it! Refuse to enter the realm of delusion like the perpetrator, or you will ultimately become sick yourself. Hold them accountable for workplace harassment and discrimination.

There are many psychologists who would deceive you into believing that racism is all in your mind, that it doesn't really exist, or that you're just paranoid. Don't believe the lie. Like slavery, they refuse to own the post-traumatic stress disorders that manifest in self-hate, low self-worth, and low self-esteem—unexplainable feelings of inferiority—which can all be attributed to a past history of suffering and harm. The greatest test is the one you give yourself. The challenge you choose to overcome.

Such massive, inconceivable post-traumatic stress disorders continue to wreak havoc on the Black community—on our health, mentally, emotionally, and otherwise—forcing us to make major mental adjustments every day to accommodate aberrant, unnatural behavior. We become mentally enslaved for life, with no one willing to discuss the topic. Instead, they slap a label on you, attempting to convince you that you're having paranoid delusions, are schizophrenic, bipolar, or antisocial. To that, I say: don't let anyone label you—especially if they're guilty of practicing racism. Refuse to wear the label.

They will fill your medical charts with labels when the diagnosis should simply read: *Undetermined.*

The truth is, you're outstanding. You're dynamic. You're brilliant. They sense it, too, just by talking to you. That's why they want to eschew your progress, discredit you, and render you unbelievable. Refuse to own the labels of your haters. It's a spiritual problem. People who are not spiritual should not be allowed to diagnose a people they neither like nor understand—and against whom they practice hate. What's gotten old is that people always want to fix *you*, never the perpetrator of the hate crime. It's easier to make *you* the problem.

Let's face it: racism is a viable topic, ripe for discussion—for the care, safety, and well-being of all people. The wall of bigotry that permeates the workforce and negatively impacts lives on college campuses and in our communities tells us plainly that it is a present-day truth. Let's stop sweeping it under the rug and get healed.

Another random poll that would be interesting is to see how many psychiatrists currently study the effects of racism on people—and how it impacts a person's life from birth to adolescence to adulthood. You won't see many Gallup polls on that. The fact that psychiatrists have chosen exclusion over inclusion fuels the fire of controversy. Exclusion is the overt refusal to take ownership, while professing to be the moral authority.

Exclusion is a cop-out. People make no attempt to address the truth of what others are being forced to live with—while being told it's somehow their fault that they're being treated inhumanely in the workplace. And believe me, some victims of workplace harassment don't handle it well at all. Some shoot up the place.

Somebody needs to put the psychiatrists themselves on the proverbial couch and ask: Why haven't you studied and researched your own motivations? Why are there no stats on the effects of racism? No doubt, it's driven by greed and money—not by a true concern for mental health, safety, or community welfare. The fact that they choose exclusion means they're part of the status quo. And those stats? They'll never be released.

It takes a great deal of energy to be totally ruthless when fabricating, manufacturing, and creating workplace harassment situations on a continual basis. Mistakes are inevitable. Keep a journal, a log. What you've got to know is that endurance is the name of the game, and the end result is knowing that your adversary will begin to make mistakes as they go about the business of plotting your demise. Trust me—it's inevitable that mistakes will be made.

I've seen it play out in the courtroom many, many times, and those mistakes ultimately lead to lawsuits. Expect your haters to entrap themselves eventually, as they formulate paperwork and create situations of workplace disharmony in order to get you disciplined or entangled in some sick plot or scheme. To them, it started out as a game. But to you—it's your destiny. Life is not a game. Relationships are not games. Love is not a game.

And I say destiny, knowing that whatever you do and say is being recorded. Pick your fights.

Know it and govern yourself accordingly—your temperament, your speech, your demeanor, your actions. Keep your words few. Keep your actions appropriate. Keep your demeanor professional at all times as you deal with negative people in the workplace. Don't forget to smile. Make a conscious effort to get a grip, take a deep breath, and know that the whole world is truly a stage, and you've got a part to play—break a leg!

But what you don't want to do is become involved in some clique, some rebel group in the workplace that sets itself up and rallies around some anti-agency movement that causes a walk-out or riot. Although there are times when defensive tactics are necessary, if you're singled out and being boxed off and targeted as an individual, it's best to stay neutral until enough mistakes have been made by the adversary, so that eventually the breadcrumb trail leads back to their own front door.

I say that literally. No one can consistently target and create workplace harassment without it eventually rolling back to where it originated. Laws of cause and effect kick in—even karma. It's like the law of gravity. The law of relativity. A boomerang effect. At the time when things appear quiet on the home front, the adversary begins to plot and scheme, not realizing that there are natural principles and forces of nature in place. For every action, there is truly a reaction.

That's why, for your own safety and well-being, you must maintain a journal or diary from day one when

168

entering the workforce on a new job. There's always going to be someone who doesn't want you there—someone who has a problem with you as a person, with how far you've come, and feels it's their duty to stop your progress. It's an inconvenient truth.

On this journey, I've found it's women versus women in the workforce—taking each other out—which is a travesty, as we all share similar backgrounds with respect to women's rights issues.

And when people generate thoughts and send out negative forces of energy against you, you need to document it—write it down. Record the date, time, and place when you have these premonitions. Something triggered it. Contrary to popular belief, some people do indeed practice witchcraft, and if you're a spiritual being, those premonitions are warnings. What seems remote now could balloon into something much larger later, possibly a loss of finances or contracts a year from now.

What I would say to you is this: just make sure you're not the instigator of the workplace harassment. That's the only way things are going to work out for your good. The greatest temptation you will ever face is to respond to hate with hate—rail for rail. Know that the positive forces of love and truth are still in full force and effect.

To this temptation, I'd say: keep your temper under control! Your control over this temptation to respond to your haters in the workplace will determine whether you eat for the next year or not—or even whether you draw unemployment if terminated. Then the roles will reverse, as you're forced to explain your actions in a sworn affidavit or statement.

It's troubled people who create hostile work environments—not mentally healthy and stable ones. Just don't you be named among the instigators, or none of this will work for you. Let them be forced to write their statements, as the pathway of truth forces them to fabricate yet another lie to explain their behavior.

I say that with forty years of courtroom drama and experience—witnessing situations where the pathway of truth from the mouths of witnesses always led back to the originator, the instigator, the creator of the workplace horror. The positive forces can and will work for you if you embrace—like a flowing stream of water—the natural laws of cause and effect.

I know it sounds bizarre, embracing life's naturally emitting forces of energy and karma, but not embracing the naturally flowing currents and energy is what leads to violence in the workplace. People take matters into their own hands when they become overwhelmed by pain and suffering, emotional stress, and despondency—when they don't know what the next step should be.

We might need to be taught this concept of calm control and rational thinking. They weren't keeping a log. They weren't keeping a journal. They didn't know how to embrace what was happening in their lives. That's why they've decided *you're* the target—you're the reason their life is so messed up.

There are zero-tolerance policies that have been implemented against workplace violence and harassment, so embrace them. They were created for out-of-control, nonsensical employees and employers who feel they are above the law.

Admittedly, the ability to act like children lies innate within us all. We are not born adults, but babies—children. So, as adults, we can only draw on our past teachings as children. As we evolve into adulthood, we should know right from wrong.

Lack of mutual respect fuels and drives bullies. The refusal to respect others is a definite red flag that you believe you're above the law or somehow have special privileges because of your personal accomplishments. We need to do better at this—so we can stop tearing up the workplace.

Workplace harassment has its consequences. As adults, when we experience mental health issues or step out of line, we don't get sent to the principal's office anymore—we get sent straight to jail, or to some EAP (Employee Assistance Program), where we can get counseling. Or we're issued some oral or written warning, reprimanded, or face disciplinary action on the job, up to and including termination, or we're RIF-ed—or even outright fired.

Workplace harassment and discrimination in the 21st century are here to stay—so look for it. And what's not often stated is that Black-on-Black hate, envy, and jealousy are the most devastating forms of hate.

I've recorded hundreds of EEOC Commission hearings over the past forty years, where workplace harassment of educated Black professionals eventually caused the person to resign, quit, and turn in their badge—while the perpetrator remained gainfully employed, simply transferring to another division and being offered a fresh start.

There are several keys to staying gainfully employed in the 21st century workplace, and these keys can only be described as vital, necessary tools of survival. It's survival of the fittest now, as we see people losing their jobs in alarming numbers across all occupations in this nation, as the dismantling of their dreams continues to rage.

SURVIVING THE GAME

You're under constant scrutiny and observation in the workplace, even though it's on the down-low. And know this: someone has already appointed themselves the judge and jury of your behavior—a gatekeeper for when and if you get out of line. They're analyzing you, trying to learn what buttons they can push that will set you off.

How do I know this? Because it's happened to me.

Most importantly, be you. Be your authentic self. Don't be coerced into acting like somebody other than yourself, or else you'll lose touch with who you really are. That's why, upon acceptance of any job, contract, bid, or award, you must implement the following steps to help you survive racism and discrimination in a hostile work environment:

Keep a journal, diary, or log of your daily challenges and events as they occur in the workplace.

Record names, dates, and times as things happen. This will help arm you when addressing any future job-related allegations involving co-workers or colleagues. Keeping a log also helps you recognize your own shortcomings and identify areas where you may need to improve your interpersonal skills. Sharpen your rough edges as you strive to do a good job. Don't be afraid to go the extra mile.

Learn how to respond appropriately to negative situations in the workplace with tact and professionalism—rather than anger, retaliation, or revenge.

When you need to respond to any job-related allegation, take the weekend to meditate and reflect on what your response should be. Even a 24-hour pause can make a huge difference. Taking time before responding can help prevent a situation from erupting into a larger workplace disruption. Workplace disruption is the number one reason people are removed from their jobs. It's often categorized as a failure to maintain a satisfactory and harmonious working relationship with the public and fellow employees. So take time to consider the appropriateness of your response.

Silence is golden. Some things are better left unsaid.

As with all jobs, you're expected to improvise until you fully understand your responsibilities. Once you've learned what's expected of you, make the necessary adjustments and build upon your training.

You overcome workplace harassment by staying focused on your job—not on peer pressure—and by exceeding expectations in work-related tasks so that your job performance is never called into question.

It doesn't hurt to have a pleasant, professional personality that fits within your niche, office, or work environment. Stay neutral. Refuse to get caught up in office politics. Don't become the class clown or the group spokesperson when dealing with personnel issues—it's a trap. You'll be the first to go. You'll have your chance to speak on your own personnel issues if and when that time presents itself—as you're being escorted out of the building.

Refuse the temptation to gossip about anyone's situation or personal circumstances. Always be supportive of group efforts, but don't be overly opinionated. Govern yourself accordingly.

You may think you got your job solely because of your degree and qualifications, but in truth, someone paved the way before you. In the 21st-century workplace, someone cut the trail, cleared the path, and fought so that you could even be considered. You didn't get there by yourself. Honor those who marched and protested for justice, who fought for affirmative action, for Equal Employment Opportunity laws, for contracting fairness, and for Diversity, Equity, and Inclusion policies that opened doors for small, woman-owned businesses and allowed people of color to become entrepreneurs. Someone died so that you could have the right to coexist in a hostile work environment. I call it "The Greatest Story Ever Told."

To the young Black professionals who are now educated and gainfully employed—I say this with love—you don't know the whole story. Many of you bask in the rewards of the Civil Rights Movement, enjoying freedoms and opportunities that were hard-fought and paid for in blood. Just because you now have the freedom to attend the college or university of your choice and walk straight into a job after graduation, don't assume that's always been the norm. A foundation was laid for that. And to you, I say—"I dare you!" Yes. I dare you to come into the workplace and insult older Black employees—those who lived through the struggle that opened the door for you—by calling them old or obsolete, and in some cases even driving them out of the workforce through age discrimination and harassment. You don't know the whole story.

If you took the time to get to know them and respect them, you'd find they possess more wisdom, knowledge, and experience than you'll ever know.

Oh, we forgive you—but learn the full story before you discount your elders in the workplace. You may ask, "What's the big deal?" I'm just saying—respect your elders. We've lost that value in the 21st-century workplace. Just because no one told you about the sit-ins, the fire hoses, the bus boycotts, the beatings, the bombings, and the assassinations doesn't mean they didn't happen. Many of us still remember it like it was yesterday—just as we remember where we were on 9/11.

So to our young adults, I say—respect your elders. They're the reason you're where you are today.

We remember the senseless killings of civil rights activists. We remember the church bombing that killed three young girls during Sunday school. We remember the lynchings, the gasoline poured on lifeless bodies, the inhumane treatment inflicted on innocent Black people—not centuries ago, but just 80 years ago.

We remember the "colored" water fountains, restrooms, restaurants, and bus sections. We remember not being allowed to stay at certain hotels.

To that I say, "I dare you!" I dare you to come in and assault your own people—Black folks—simply for succeeding and defying the odds. We've come a long way, and we must never forget the price that was paid. We must always honor and respect those who went before us and gave their lives to create opportunities for future generations.

That's why there's no place for workplace harassment, racism, and discrimination among Black people in the workplace. There's a silent war being fought right now, as individuals bring their personal histories and childhood upbringings into the workforce. These unresolved issues often manifest in the loss of jobs and contracts, as the workplace becomes a battleground for the expression of pent-up frustration and displaced childhood trauma. To that, I say: hold them accountable.

I say that respectfully—learn how to work within the system. Know that the day of trouble is coming, and your best defense will be to arm yourself with a Civil Rights attorney or an employment lawyer, along with your journals, diary, or daily logbook. Make the system work for you by holding wrongdoers accountable. Losing a job can feel comparable to death itself, as you grieve the loss of your home, your car, your freedom, and your ability to move freely in your daily life. Know that you may suffer great loss—but there's nothing like being prepared.

One could only wish that the demonstrators and marchers of the '60s had taken time to pen a manuscript, a book, or a memoir—a guide, if you will—for the next generations to follow. A practical self-help book for dealing with feelings of hopelessness and despair in the 21st-century workplace, as we navigate desperate times against the walls set up to block our success.

Learn how to fight for your rights—not with guns and knives, but with facts, dates, timelines, evidence, and testimony from witnesses. This means you've got to keep a cool head throughout the process. That's the only way to change things for the next generation. Racism and discrimination are not dead—they're alive and well. They just wear different hats or go by different names, such as *workplace harassment.*

Workplace harassment, intimidation, and bullying are the new hate crimes. That's why they must be fought in a court of law. Like cigarettes, they're the silent killers—but without documentation and evidence, proving your case will be difficult.

Fighting workplace harassment is not for the fainthearted or the fearful. And everyone is betting that you don't have the financial means to pay for a legal defense. So, no matter what you do, you lose—and are forced to carry the bitterness for the rest of your life. That is, unless you develop the psychological strength and skills to at least maneuver through it, overcome it, or become submissive enough to your tormentor to survive it and move on. As quiet as it's kept, in the 21st-century workplace—like rape—we all know someone who is a victim or has been a victim of their co-workers. And for whatever reason, no one wants to get involved.

Employees caught participating in workplace harassment and discrimination should be terminated—not only because they disrupt the workplace, but because they cost millions of dollars in litigation and lost revenue. Not to mention, it's time-consuming. Workplace harassment, simply put, is a form of bullying—psychological warfare. And bullying is often a manifestation of childhood trauma or behavior disorders, which ultimately evolves into racism when carried into adulthood and brought into the workplace. It begs the question: what kind of sick pleasure could a logical, rational-thinking, God-fearing person derive from destroying another human being?

Learn how to psychologically profile prospective co-workers—they're profiling you. Ask the pertinent questions: How well do they relate to people in general? Have they participated in any hate crimes in the past? When interacting with new people in the workplace, reserve judgment until you've observed how they interact with others and had a chance to weigh their motives and intentions—especially in how they treat you and your peers. This is exactly why the 90-day probationary period was created. It won't take long before you become proficient at assessing who you can and cannot allow into your space. And know this: Black folks are just as guilty of this conduct in the workplace as any other race. It's a crisis of the spirit.

There ought to be questions asked on job applications or during interviews that address these very issues: Do you work well with other races? Have you worked in a diverse workforce before? Have you been found guilty of committing a hate crime against a person of a different race, origin, creed, or ethnicity in the past five years? If so, explain. Have you ever had a workplace harassment complaint filed against you by anyone of another race in the past five years? If so, explain. Questions like these would stop a lot of the nonsense that goes on in the workplace.

You may think it could never happen to you, but the reality is that there are people in the workplace who feel obligated—who carry a sense of duty and responsibility, even an inalienable right—to sabotage your career. It's a twisted form of allegiance.

I'd like to take a poll to see how many folks are guilty of, have in the past engaged in, or are currently involved in workplace harassment of a coworker. I'd bet it'd be an alarming statistic. Now *that's* a poll you'll never see on the front page of *News Weekly*. We tend to hide this behavior when it comes to adults. No one wants others to know we're capable of acting this way. Haters collaborate— even though they are employees themselves. But the fact that you've become a target of their hate means they've formed a preconceived idea about who you are and where, in their opinion, you should be relegated. They don't care about your merit or superior skill sets. They're in it for the camaraderie, the bond, the sisterhood—jealous women, often with unresolved self-worth issues.

It becomes: *I carry more worth than you,* and they attempt to prove it by inflicting harassment upon you. Their lack of fulfillment in their own lives causes your success to feel like an attack on their self-image. Rather than striving for higher excellence, they react destructively. To that I say: **keep shining**. Don't let jealousy dim your light.

In closing, my message is this: it's going to happen for the rest of your life, so learn how to fight back. Start by aligning yourself with the Word of God.

Sometimes I think that's why life sends us problems in the first place—to teach us how to fight back. Throughout life, you'll find people who respect you and others who couldn't care less about you, your spouse, your kids, your home, or your dreams. To them, you're not indispensable. The rules that got you to the top suddenly change. You're treated with disrespect, even inhumanely. Just give it some time—soon you'll see things begin to deteriorate at work. You'll find yourself asking, *What did I do? I didn't do anything wrong,* as you're escorted out of the building.

When that happens, you've got to stop and take legal action. Hold them accountable—that's the only language some people understand.

Create a personal legal defense fund. Set aside money each month for potential legal expenses. This group hates exposure—so take them to court. And if you fail to document your experiences, nothing you say in court will matter. **Let the evidence speak for itself.**

The judicial system is brutal. It's a beast. In my business, I've had numerous lawyers steal from me—transcript copies—and then spread lies among their colleagues, accusing me of theft. Some didn't want to pay fair per-page rates, or because I was Black, they believed they could dictate what they wanted to pay, regardless of what was standard or ethical.

Yes, we're living in troubled times, and the only way to survive racism in the workplace is to get everything in writing. Contracts and agreements—without fail—must be documented. Don't trust oral or verbal promises, not even from family or loved ones. After forty years of working in the system, I've seen families implode—shooting and killing each other, just like Cain and Abel. It happens.

Additionally, seek out and build relationships with like-minded individuals—preferably Christians who are of kindred spirit, rather than basing connections solely on race. Through everything I've experienced with haters, racism, walls of division, and hypocrisy, I've learned there are still good people in every race. And conversely, there are bad people in every race too.

For every Jekyll and Hyde I encountered, I also found many White colleagues, associates, and clients who had no problem working with a minority contractor and were not racially divisive or motivated by hate. To them, I say thank you—I honor your integrity.

We live in a racially complex society that is difficult to navigate—in the workplace, at church, and in our communities. We are all searching for a place where we can feel welcomed—a place where we can be our authentic selves.

Over the past forty years, I've managed to find and build working relationships with people who didn't think like those I considered haters. It's up to you to explore the possibility of establishing relationships with individuals you deem worthwhile—those who share your values and ideals. Don't leave it merely to chance. Be open to all areas of growth and development as you climb the corporate ladder on your way to financial freedom.

The struggle continues. You must develop the gift of discernment so as not to become entangled with people who don't mean you any good—not just in the workplace, but also at church and in your community. They will set you back and delay your dreams and aspirations.

Life becomes easier when you walk side-by-side with colleagues and associates with whom you share a spiritual connection—people with common goals, values, and passions. When you are connected to others in this way, it's easier to be yourself. The pressure to conform fades.

I would submit that *you* are Rosa Parks. *You* are Dr. Martin Luther King Jr. *You* are Malcolm X. *You* are the Medgar Evers of the 21st-century workplace.

The ability to make history didn't end with the deaths of our Civil Rights leaders. That was just the beginning. Their legacy was left for *you*. You are—and will be, every day of your life—creating and making history. Don't let anyone tell you that their deaths marked the end of our ability to dream.

History is a continuum. As long as there is life, there will be history. God is the author and Creator of history.

History-making moments present themselves daily. It's up to each of us to step up and make a difference. Dare to be different. The courage to make a difference is not given by the hand of God to the fainthearted. You were created and chosen for a mission—a divine assignment that is uniquely yours. For the rest of your life, you are charged with making a difference.

To that end, I'd say: on this planet, we must all learn to work together, live together, coexist together—and yes, when necessary, even tolerate one another—as we pass through this portal of time called life. We are all passing through this marvelous gift called life before we move on to the final frontier: eternal life. Some of us will live to be forty, fifty, or even a hundred years old. Others may die at birth. But whatever time we're given, let's learn to be team players—in the workplace and in our communities—so that whatever time we have left on this earth, we can live it to the fullest. Let's enjoy the ride, enjoy the journey, and live long and prosper, rather than making it difficult for others to succeed, enjoy the fruits of their labor, and accomplish their goals.

In closing, life is a gift. Make the best of it. It's not all good. It's not all bad. It's not all ugly. But life is best defined by how you deal with and respond to the adversities that come your way. Responding appropriately to life's challenges promotes positive growth and experience, which will ultimately endow you with wisdom, knowledge, and understanding as you discover God's intended purpose for your life. And with all of its devastation, you'll find that the human spirit is not easily broken—but rather resilient and pliable, able to bounce back under even the most extraordinary circumstances that life sends your way.

That is what it means to survive the game.

Making A Difference! I was chosen for this!

Author, Entrepreneur, Evangelist of Shield of Faith Outreach Ministry,

Dr. Belinda D. Moore, LCR, CCR